F. Scott Fitzgerald's St. Paul Plays

1911-1914

F. Scott Fitzgerald's St. Paul Plays 1911-1914

Edited with an Introduction by
ALAN MARGOLIES

PRINCETON, NEW JERSEY
PRINCETON UNIVERSITY LIBRARY
1978

Library of Congress Card No. 78-56379
ISBN No. 0-87811-022-4

Published under the sponsorship of
the Friends of the Princeton University Library

Designed by Frank Mahood

Printed in the United States of America
by Princeton University Press
at Princeton, New Jersey

Acknowledgements

I WISH to thank the staff of the Minnesota Historical Society, New York Public Library, and Princeton University Library for much assistance. In particular at Princeton University Library I am grateful to Alexander P. Clark, Alexander Wainwright, Mary Ann Jensen, Mardel Pacheco, and Charles E. Greene, as well as Wanda Randall, formerly of the Library, and G. E. Bentley of the Friends of the Princeton University Library. Among those in the St. Paul area who assisted me I wish in particular to thank Lloyd Hackl, Barbara Lechner, Louise Rosel, and Toni Thornton. I am especially indebted to Mr. and Mrs. Norris D. Jackson for many favors. Others who helped me include Jackson Bryer, Don L. Cook, Carol Irish, Ralph Magoffin, Jean Merritt, Peter Shillingsburg, and Chester Seims. Finally, Matthew J. Bruccoli answered many questions and made many valuable suggestions. I am particularly grateful to him.

A grant from the John Jay College Small Grants Program was especially helpful. I also wish to acknowledge grant assistance from the American Council of Learned Societies and the Research Foundation of the City University of New York.

The plays in this edition are published with the permission of Harold Ober Associates, Incorporated. Publication and performance rights remain the property of Frances Fitzgerald Smith.

All illustrations are from The Fitzgerald Papers, Princeton University Library.

Acknowledgments

Contents

F. Scott Fitzgerald's St. Paul Plays

1911-1914

Introduction

ON AUGUST 8 and 9, 1911, in St. Paul, Minnesota, at the St. Paul Academy, then on Dale Street and Portland Avenue, a group of young friends who lived in the Summit Avenue area presented a theatrical performance for the benefit of the city's Protestant Orphan Asylum. A brief curtain raiser, *A Pair of Lunatics*, starring two of the youngsters, Dorothy Greene and Scott Fitzgerald (who would celebrate his fifteenth birthday the next month), was followed by magic tricks performed by a third youngster, Gustave Schurmeier. This, in turn, was followed by the major attraction, John Madison Morton's *A Regular Fix*, a comedy with a cast of ten including Fitzgerald in a minor role.

The group quickly grew to some forty members and soon was the Elizabethan Dramatic Club, named—according to a news clipping in Fitzgerald's scrapbook in Princeton University Library—for its "directress," Elizabeth Clay Rogers Magoffin, who had just turned twenty that previous March. Attorney Samuel McAfee Magoffin, her father, claimed two governors of Kentucky as ancestors, and her mother, Elizabeth Moran Rogers Magoffin, could boast of such distinguished forebears as Thomas Dudley, first governor of Massachusetts, Henry Clay, and George Rogers Clark. The Magoffin home, at 540 Summit, was less than two blocks from the Academy and not much further in a slightly different direction from Holly Avenue where the Fitzgeralds lived from 1909 to 1914. When the novelist's family finally moved to Summit Avenue, first to 593 in 1914 and then to 599 in 1918 ("In a house below the average / Of a street above the average," he was to write),[1] they were just a block or so away from the Magoffins. But Fitzgerald's association in the drama club with Elizabeth Clay Rogers Magoffin was, so far as is known, the only major link between the two families.

It was in the Magoffin home in August, 1911, that the Eliza-

[1] Fitzgerald to Alida Bigelow, September 22, 1919, in *The Letters of F. Scott Fitzgerald*, ed. Andrew Turnbull (New York: Scribners, 1963), p. 456.

bethan Dramatic Club, during its organizational meeting, performed *The Girl from Lazy J*, Fitzgerald's first effort for the group. The play was brief and extremely flawed. Yet, the performance signalled an important event for the young playwright who had also appeared in the leading role. "I begin to get my head turned," he wrote in his scrapbook between the programs for *A Regular Fix* and this latest production. And, undoubtedly, Elizabeth Magoffin further contributed to these feelings of pride when she gave him a photograph that year inscribed "To Scott 'He had that Spark— Magnetic Mark—' With the best love of the one who thinks so," as well as a poem including a line explaining that "the Spark is a gift, and a part of our God."[2]

During each of the following three summers, an Elizabethan Dramatic Club production of a Fitzgerald play was performed for charity. While each was a great improvement over Fitzgerald's first effort, and while the last two, especially, were applauded in newspaper accounts of the group's activities, none was a polished, mature work. The reader should not expect anything like the novelist's professional efforts. In these plays, however, one will find the talent and enthusiasm of the boy who would grow up to become one of America's greatest writers.

Though born in St. Paul in 1896, Fitzgerald had spent much of the first twelve years of his life in New York State, his family first having moved to Buffalo in 1898, then to Syracuse in 1901, and then back to Buffalo in 1903. Finally, in 1908, after his father Edward Fitzgerald was dismissed from Procter and Gamble, the firm for whom he had worked during this period, the Fitzgeralds returned to St. Paul.

Fitzgerald's *Ledger*, the outline chart of his life probably first begun in 1919 or 1920, records some of his early flirtations with the stage. "He remembers the attic where he had a red sash with which he acted Paul Revere," a note for his seventh year states.[3] Another note, this time for September, 1906, when he was ten, tells us "He made up shows in Dugham's attic, all based on The American Revolution and a red sash and three cornered hat." Four months later, his family was taking advan-

[2] The photograph and poem are in Fitzgerald's scrapbook at Princeton University Library.

[3] All Ledger citations are from *F. Scott Fitzgerald's Ledger: A Facsimile* (Washington, D.C.: Bruccoli Clark/Microcard Editions, 1972).

tage of his exhibitionistic streak. Of this time he wrote, "His mother got the idea he could sing so he performed 'Way down in colon town' and 'Don't get married any more' for all visitors." Meanwhile, during the years 1906 through 1908, he was attending many of the stock company performances in Buffalo with his friend Hamilton Wende, and according to Andrew Turnbull, reenacting a good number of these performances for the neighborhood children. Then, after his family returned to St. Paul, he attended many of the vaudeville shows at the Orpheum Theatre, again reenacting what he had seen.[4] Further, he continued to write plays. In 1909, he constructed a half hour drama titled *Arsène Lupin*, based on the adventures of the popular detective character of the day, hand lettered cards of admission referring to himself as "stageman," and presented the play in the living room of his friend Teddy Ames.[5] And a *Ledger* note for the following year tells of a "Play in Cecil's attic." In addition, at the St. Paul Academy between 1909 and 1911 he participated in debates, recitations, and dramatic exercises. One news article in his scrapbook, for example, tells of a "literary meeting" at the school on May 12 of his final year during which he and Teddy Ames imitated stage personalities Montgomery and Stone singing "Travel, Travel Little Star."

Of course, to emphasize Fitzgerald's interest in theatre too much during these early years is to create a distortion. As the notes for the *Ledger* testify, his youthful literary zeal manifested itself in many areas. A note for January, 1907, for example, states: "He began a history of the U.S. and also a detective story about a necklace that was hidden in a trap door under the carpet. Wrote celebrated essay on George Washington & St. Ignatius." Another, this time for June, 1909, states: "Wrote The Mystery of the Raymond Mortgage. Also 'Elavo' (or was that in Buffalo) and a complicated story of some knights." He summed up this activity in a note for January, 1911, referring to himself as an "inveterate author." During the 1909-10 and 1910-11 school years, while he was attending St. Paul Academy, four of his short stories, "The Mystery of the Raymond Mortgage," "Reade, Substitute Right Half," "A Debt of Honor,"

[4] Andrew Turnbull, *Scott Fitzgerald* (New York: Scribners, 1962), pp. 12 and 25.

[5] Fitzgerald's scrapbook.

and "The Room With the Green Blinds," as well as a news article, appeared in *Now and Then*, the St. Paul Academy magazine. During the following two school years, while he was attending the Newman School in Hackensack, New Jersey, three more stories, "A Luckless Santa Claus," "Pain and the Scientist," and "The Trail of the Duke," as well as "Football," a poem, and at least two news articles in addition were published in the *Newman News*.

But at the St. Paul Academy, Fitzgerald's theatre activity had impressed one of his teachers most of all. "I imagined he would become an actor of the variety type," wrote C.N.B. Wheeler years later.[6] Further, Fitzgerald's literary activity during the summers between 1911 and 1914 seems to have been devoted mainly to his work with the Elizabethan Dramatic Club. After that first year at the Newman School, during which he attended many shows in New York (*The Little Millionaire*, *The Quaker Girl*, *Over the River*, and *The Private Secretary* are mentioned in his *Ledger*), he returned to St. Paul with his next play—"wrote it on a train," he said in the *Ledger*—*The Captured Shadow*.

"ENTER SUCCESS!," he wrote in his scrapbook next to the clippings for *The Captured Shadow*. Once again he played the leading role, this time that of a gentleman burglar. The play was performed before a paying audience on August 23, 1912, at the Oak Hall school for girls on Holly Street, only a short walk from Fitzgerald's home, and there were many rewards. The show had raised sixty dollars for the Baby Welfare Association. For the cast there was dinner the preceding evening at the Schurmeier home, then a theatre party, a hayrack party, and dinner at the Town and Country Club during the afternoon and evening following the performance. And for Fitzgerald and his friends there was much favorable publicity. As was the custom for such charity activities, especially when some of the youngsters were the children of prominent St. Paul residents, most of the notices appeared in the society section of the local newspapers. A reviewer stated, "Much comment was elicited by the young author's cleverness as well as by the remarkable amateur work accompanied by the others in the cast."[7]

[6] Turnbull, *Scott Fitzgerald*, p. 20.

[7] The clippings are in Fitzgerald's scrapbook.

The following year, on April 28, at the Trinity Lyceum in Hackensack, the Newman School Comedy Club presented a double bill, *The Power of Music* and David Garrick's version of *The Taming of the Shrew*. In the opener, Fitzgerald had the role of a king whose son eventually succeeds as concert violinist despite the opposition of the court. Next to the program in his scrapbook, Fitzgerald wrote, "the young king à la Donald Bryan," an allusion to the popular musical comedy star. Then four months later, his third Elizabethan Dramatic Club play, *Coward*, a Civil War tale, received even more newspaper acclaim than *The Captured Shadow*. (A few of these accounts, some advertisements, and the *Ledger* for July, 1913, refer to it as *The Coward*.) In his scrapbook, Fitzgerald wrote, "—THE GREAT EVENT—." Not only was he the author again, but now he had *two* parts, one as brother of the heroine, the other, a minor role as a Union soldier who attempts to steal her necklace; in addition, he was now listed in the program as "Stage Manager." Finally, because of the turnout at the performance on August 29, 1913, at the downtown Y. W. C. A. auditorium—"a large and fashionable audience," according to a reviewer—and because of the $150 raised for the Baby Welfare Association, it was accorded a second showing on September 2 at the White Bear Yacht Club in Dellwood, some twelve miles away. Here, after being treated to dinner, the cast performed to an audience of 300 more.[8]

Fitzgerald entered Princeton that fall and he soon became active in the Triangle Club. He submitted lyrics for the 1913-14 show, and, when they were not accepted, he helped out at rehearsals. In addition, he began working on the show for the following year, *Fie! Fie! Fi-Fi!*, for which he was eventually to receive credit for writing the lyrics and claimed, in addition, to have written the book. Then, at the end of the school year, he returned home, this time for his final Elizabethan Dramatic Club play, *Assorted Spirits*.

Once again Fitzgerald was applauded in the local newspapers for his work. "Scott Fitzgerald, the 17-year-old playwright . . . turned out a roaring farce and is clever throughout," wrote one reviewer. And once again Fitzgerald not only had a major role, this time that of Peter Wetherby, the owner of the house that

[8] Ibid.

is haunted by the "assorted spirits," but he also again was listed as "Stage Manager." The first performance, on August 8, 1914, at the Y. W. C. A. auditorium raised $300 for the Baby Welfare Association and another performance the following night at the White Bear Yacht Club garnered another $200. It was during the first act of this second performance before a crowd of 200 that the light fuses blew, explosions were heard, and the house was plunged into darkness. All of this happened just as one of the actors costumed as a devil had made his entrance, and this apparently only added to the fears of the more impressionable in the audience. Fitzgerald averted panic when he "proved equal to the situation, however, and leaping to the edge of the stage," according to a newspaper article, "quieted the audience with an improvised monologue."[9]

After the demise of the Elizabethan Dramatic Club, Fitzgerald, of course, continued to remain active in theatre at Princeton, where he wrote the lyrics for two more Triangle productions, *The Evil Eye* (1915-16) and *Safety First* (1916-17). In addition, he contributed two short plays to the *Nassau Literary Magazine*, "Shadow Laurels," published in April, 1915, and "The Debutante," January, 1917. But he was also writing short stories, humorous articles and sketches, poems, and jokes for the *Nassau Literary Magazine* and the *Princeton Tiger*, and while still at Princeton began the first version of the novel that eventually would be *This Side of Paradise*. Only once again would he devote any extended length of time to the theatre, and that to his political satire, *The Vegetable*, that closed after a brief tryout in Atlantic City in 1923. His papers at Princeton University Library contain hints of later attempts at writing other full length plays, but none was ever completed.

But the early theatre experience was always an important influence on Fitzgerald as a writer of fiction. From his two early novels, *This Side of Paradise* and *The Beautiful and Damned*, with their scenes in play form, to *The Great Gatsby*, a dramatic novel with dramatic scenes, limited point of view, and a time scheme superimposed upon a dramatic curve, to his unfinished final novel, *The Last Tycoon*, planned to fit a five-act formula, Fitzgerald never forgot what he had learned as a playwright.

[9] Ibid.

Further, he used some of the events from this early experience in a number of stories, most specifically in the 1928 Basil Duke Lee tale, "The Captured Shadow." Here he blended a number of events from 1911 to 1914 to create a story that gives the reader a sense of Fitzgerald's capacity in the Elizabethan Dramatic Club. In many ways, the almost sixteen-year-old playwright Basil Duke Lee is the young Fitzgerald and Riply Buckner is the young Gustave Schurmeier, his friend. Basil's methods in writing his play may be a clue to help us understand Fitzgerald's early methods. For humor Basil relies heavily on a collection of joke books and a "Treasury of Wit and Humor." Plots are based vaguely on New York shows. "This had been a season of 'crook comedies' in New York," Fitzgerald wrote of Basil's desire to write a play, "and the feel, the swing, the exact and vivid image of the two he had seen, were in the foreground of his mind. At the time they had been enormously suggestive, opening out into a world much larger and more brilliant than themselves that existed outside their windows and beyond their doors, and it was this suggested world rather than any conscious effort to imitate 'Officer 666,' that had inspired the effort before him."[10]

And if Miss Halliburton in this short story is modelled upon Elizabeth Magoffin, then the latter's function in the Elizabethan Dramatic Club, especially after the first year, may not have been too large. "I'll be the business manager and you'll direct the play, just like we said," Riply advises Basil, "but it would be good to have her there for prompter and to keep order at rehearsals. The girls' mothers'll like it."[11] Both Arthur Mizener and Andrew Turnbull, Fitzgerald's biographers, agree with this view of Elizabeth Magoffin, Turnbull in particular referring to the young Fitzgerald as the "mainspring" of the drama group.[12]

On May 22, 1914, some three months before the final Elizabethan Dramatic Club production, Elizabeth Magoffin directed a cast of Camp Fire Girls and Y. M. C. A. boys at the St. Paul Y. W. C. A. in a pageant depicting the past, present, and future

[10] F. Scott Fitzgerald, *Taps at Reveille* (New York: Scribners, 1960), p. 72.

[11] Ibid., p. 74.

[12] Arthur Mizener, *The Far Side of Paradise*, rev. ed. (Boston: Houghton Mifflin, 1965), p. 47, and Turnbull, *Scott Fitzgerald*, p. 43.

of St. Paul. The text was her 520-line poem "Saint Paul, Minnesota," a nondescript work privately published later that year.[13] A local newspaper referred politely to the pageant, giving it little of the praise bestowed on the Fitzgerald plays.[14] During the following years, Miss Magoffin continued her interests in drama and in 1929 and 1930 participated in the formation of one of the very early little theatre groups in the area, the St. Paul Players. After her marriage to Peter Garnett in 1935, she eventually left St. Paul, and then, after the death of her husband, she moved in the early 1940s to Lexington, Kentucky, where she resided until her death in 1951. Throughout this period she retained her transcriptions of the four Fitzgerald plays—in all probability the promptbooks used during the performances—as well as Fitzgerald's holograph manuscript of *The Girl from Lazy J* and the few leaves in his hand from *Coward*. A friend remembers Elizabeth Magoffin Garnett, during the latter part of her life, proudly recalling her association with the young Fitzgerald, referring to his early brilliance, and reading aloud from the plays.[15] In 1952, Princeton University Library obtained these materials from members of Elizabeth Magoffin Garnett's family.

[13] A copy of the privately printed poem as well as a carbon typescript, both with corrections in Elizabeth Magoffin's hand, are in the Minnesota Historical Society, St. Paul, Minnesota.

[14] *St. Paul Pioneer Press*, May 23, 1914, p. 11.

[15] Members of the Magoffin family, including Chester Seims of Darien, Connecticut, and Ralph Magoffin of Columbia, South Carolina, provided me with some of the information about Elizabeth Magoffin's background. Mrs. Jean Merritt of Lexington, Kentucky, recalled the event described above.

The Girl from Lazy J

FAULTS abound in this trivial first exercise, presented during the first meeting of the Elizabethan Dramatic Club. Some of the dialogue, for example, such as Leticia Larned's long-winded speech to the villain, "Now Tony Gonzoles, alias Dead Shot Hoskins, what are you doing here at this time of night?" and his reply, "I may ask the same question to you, Miss," is far too stilted. And shifts in subject are made too obvious by such clichés as "by the way" and "and say." Further, too much of the plot is unbelievable. One questions, for example, why Tony, after five years, is still carrying the blackmail letters on his person, and how it is possible for Jack Darcy not to have recognized at least the voice of the masked Leticia, his fiancée.

And yet, in Jack's awe of a prestigious Eastern school and his willingness to give up his goal for the girl he loves, one senses themes that Fitzgerald would develop in the future. In addition, in Fitzgerald's successful use of suspense—from the opening lines where Jack worries about his mother's reaction to his engagement, to the unfolding of the major plot with suggestions of Tony's evil nature, to the arrival of the disguised Leticia—there is a glimpse of a technique refined in the remaining St. Paul plays.

Parenthetically, one can only wonder if, during the year of his death, Fitzgerald recalled the hero's name here when he chose a similar one as a pseudonym. Concerning the short story finally titled "Three Hours Between Planes," he wrote Arnold Gingrich at *Esquire*: "Why don't you publish it under a pseudonym—say John Darcy. I'm awfully tired of being Scott Fitzgerald anyway as there doesn't seem to be so much money in it and I'd like to find out if people read me just because I am Scott Fitzgerald or, what is more likely, don't read me for the same reason."[1]

[1] Arnold Gingrich, Introduction, *The Pat Hobby Stories* by F. Scott Fitzgerald (New York: Scribners, 1962), pp. xvi-xvii.

The Girl from Lazy J

SCENE

Living room of the "◇O" Ranch in Texas

TIME

11:45 to 12:15 at night

CAST OF CHARACTERS

MR. GEORGE KENDALL, *owner of the "Diamond O" Ranch*	Ed. Power
MRS. KENDALL, *his wife*	M. Armstrong
JACK DARCY, *his nephew from Frisco* . . .	S. Fitzgerald
LETICIA LARNED, *a cowgirl*	D. Greene
TONY GONZOLES, *a Mexican cowpuncher* . .	R. Washington

(*Curtain rises, showing Jack in chair, whistling.*)

JACK: Accepted, accepted, by jingo, by the prettiest girl this side of the Mississippi. (*Looks at picture.*) Look at her. She's a daisy. But I wonder what Mother will say. And say, I can just see Father's face when he hears of it. But why should they care? Lord knows she's a fine girl and I'm willing to give up Yale for Leticia. Why, put her in a decent dress and she'd be the belle of the country. My, I'm tired, but I know I can't sleep thinking of this. If Mother says no, I'll be all broken up. (*Noise outside. Rises.*) What's that? A row I guess. Probably Uncle's after one of the men. (*Yawns, calls.*) Tony, Tony! I wonder where that lazy greaser is.

(*Enter Mr. Kendall, kicking Tony before him.*)

KENDALL: You will try to whip those horses, hey, you measly Mexican scoundrel? Didn't I tell you, Tony, that the next time you laid a hand to them I'd skin you? I ought by rights to put a bullet through your low down yellow hide. Now git, before I let daylight through you. Wait a minute. (*To Jack.*) Did you want him for anything?

JACK: (*To Tony.*) Tell José he can turn in now. It's almost twelve. (*Exit Tony.*)

KENDALL: What do you think, Jack. I just went out to the stable and found him beating Dolly. I think I taught him a lesson. He won't be licking my horses in a hurry again.

JACK: I don't like the looks of that fellow and you'd better be careful with these Mexicans, Uncle. They'd as soon knife a man as they would a dog and Tony's no exception to the general rule.

KENDALL: Huh! They're only good for beating horses. They haven't got enough grit to tackle a white man. But that fellow's been acting queerly for some time with the horses and I think I'll discharge him tomorrow. Jim and José can do the work, if you and I do a little extra.

JACK: Sure. By the way, I've seen him hanging around at the Lazy J. Maybe he's got some business with Mrs. Larned.

KENDALL: Oh you young scamp! What have you been doing at the Lazy J? Stuck on Leticia, hey? And say, I've got a note here that I received this afternoon. I don't know whether to take it as a joke or not.

JACK: Let's see it. (*Reads.*) "Mr. Kendall, I warn you that on the night of August 12 I will relieve you of the five thousand dollars that you received last week in payment for the yearling steers. Yours very sincerely—D. S. H." Well of all things! I think I'll keep this for a curiosity.

KENDALL: Well, what do you think I ought to do about it? Just let it go?

JACK: Do about it? There's nothing to be done.

KENDALL: But look. It says on the night of the twelfth and this is the twelfth.

JACK: (*Looks at paper.*) So it does.

KENDALL: You don't really think he'll come?

JACK: Not exactly. But you want me to sit up and await developments.

KENDALL: Well I allow I'd sleep a bit easier if you did.

JACK: All right, Uncle. (*Looks at watch.*) Why it's a quarter to twelve now. This may be only a joke but we might as well be on the safe side. Is the money in this cabinet?

KENDALL: Yes, and you'll find some cigarettes on the shelf and there's magazines so you can make yourself comfortable. And by the way, we might as well not say anything about it to Mrs. Kendall.

JACK: Very well. Good night.

KENDALL: Good night. And if you feel sleepy, don't hesitate to take a nap. (*Exit.*)

(*Enter Mrs. Kendall. Sees Jack.*)

MRS. KENDALL: How soon are you going to bed, Jack?

JACK: Just a little while, Auntie.

MRS. KENDALL: (*She begins to lock the windows.*) Hello! Someone has been tampering with this catch. It won't lock. Well I don't suppose it makes any difference.

JACK: Auntie, I've got something to tell you.

MRS. KENDALL: What is it?

JACK: I'm engaged.

MRS. KENDALL: You're engaged? Jack, you're fooling.

JACK: No, that's the truth.

MRS. KENDALL: Jack, what will your mother say?

JACK: Mother will like her, I know.

MRS. KENDALL: Tell me, who are you engaged to?

JACK: Her name is Leticia.

MRS. KENDALL: Leticia Larned?

JACK: The same.

MRS. KENDALL: Well Jack, you'll be the death of me yet. But I can't find it in my heart to be angry with you. Leticia is a fine girl.

JACK: She's the best girl in the world and, Auntie, here's her picture.

MRS. KENDALL: Well so long as you have to get married some time, I suppose I ought to be satisfied since you've picked out a nice girl. Still it does shock a body to learn it so suddenly. Well, good night. Come up when you're ready and be sure and put out all the candles. (*Exit.*)

JACK: She took it better than I expected her to. Here's hoping Mother will be as easily pacified. (*Walks to window and looks out.*) My, it's a dreary night. Hello! Auntie was right. This catch has been tampered with. I half believe there's something in this, and I've got a hunch that that rascal Tony's at the bottom of it. First, the way he's been acting today. He seems to think he's got a grudge against us and is taking it out on the horses. And he's always hanging around the Lazy J. Then the note. And finally this lock. I wonder what the initials "D. S. H." stand for.

I feel the solution lies in those three letters. (*He sits in chair, yawns and goes to sleep. Enter Tony, sneaks around, ties him, and goes out after snuffing candle. Jack wakes up but finds himself tied and helpless. The window slowly opens and Leticia enters, masked. She looks around her but does not see Jack. The door opens and Tony enters and begins to work on the cabinet. She hides behind chair. She draws revolver and steps forward.*)

LETICIA: Hands up.

(*Tony turns around startled and throws up hands.*)

Now Tony Gonzoles, alias Dead Shot Hoskins, what are you doing here at this time of night?

TONY: I may ask the same question to you, Miss—

LETICIA: Hush! Not a word from you. You probably know why I came here tonight. Where are the letters you stole from my mother five years ago? You blackmailer. Hand them to me now or, as I live, you'll die. I'll give you three. One— Two— Thank you. (*Burns them.*) And now as I have accomplished my purpose, I think I'll lace you up a bit to keep you out of mischief. (*Ties him and starts for door with revolver in holster.*)

(*Enter Mr. Kendall.*)

KENDALL: By all that's holy, it's a woman! Well Miss D. S. H., or whatever your initials are, your game is up. I've got you with the goods. Let's have that gun. You got two of 'em tied up, eh? Well you are a plucky one.

LETICIA: (*Noticing Jack. Aside.*) It's Jack. How shall I explain my presence here?

(*Mr. Kendall unties Gonzoles, who starts for door. Unties Jack, who starts towards Gonzoles.*)

JACK: So you're a blackmailer as well as a robber. Yes, I heard it all. Take that! (*They fire. Gonzoles falls.*) Uncle, put away your gun. I don't know who that girl is, but whoever she is, she has saved my life tonight, for Tony, or rather Hoskins, would have stabbed me before he made his getaway. (*Walks toward Leticia.*) Well whoever you are, you're going to shed that mask now.

(*Enter Mrs. Kendall, with telegram.*)

MRS. KENDALL: Here's a telegram for you, Jack. (*Sees Tony on floor.*) Oh, what's this!

JACK: (*Opens telegram and reads.*) "Mr. Jack Darcy, '◇O' Ranch —I consent to your marriage. Go ahead. Mrs. Larned an old school friend of mine. Congratulations. Mother." (*Looks up; in astonishment, sees that masked girl, who has now unmasked, is Leticia.*)

(*Starts back.*) Leticia!

LETICIA: Jack!

KENDALL: God bless you, my children.

(*Curtain.*)

Description of Furnishings: Interior of rancher's shack. Lights dim. Some candles. Rustic furniture and hangings—elk horns, Mexican baskets, blankets, etc.— Two chairs, a table, and a lounge. Door at L. Cabinet at R. Window at C.

Properties of Characters:

Jack Darcy— Girl's picture.
Leticia Larned— Mask; rope; revolver.
Mr. Kendall— Note; revolver.
Mrs. Kendall— Telegram.
Tony Gonzoles— Shotgun; rope; packet of letters.

The Captured Shadow

WHILE Paul Armstrong's *Alias Jimmy Valentine* may have been one of the inspirations for *The Captured Shadow*, as Fitzgerald himself suggested to a newspaper interviewer in 1922,[1] the only similarities between the two plays are the assumed identities of the heroes and the fact that both are gentlemen. *Alias Jimmy Valentine* was about a safecracker who reforms and then risks being returned to prison on an old charge when he rescues a young girl suffocating in a locked safe. *The Captured Shadow*, on the other hand, was far closer in plot to the Arsène Lupin stories that Fitzgerald had been reading. The young playwright may also have been influenced by the stage rendition of *Arsène Lupin* credited to Francis de Croisset and Maurice Leblanc which toured the country after its New York production in 1909. There are resemblances between it and *The Captured Shadow*, and while there is no proof that Fitzgerald saw this play, Amory Blaine in *This Side of Paradise* attends two performances of *Arsène Lupin* in Minneapolis.

But no matter what he used as model or models for this second play for the Elizabethan Dramatic Club, Fitzgerald's scriptwork had improved remarkably since *The Girl from Lazy J*. His characterizations were far more interesting. Here he contrasted a bumbling detective, Inspector Leon Dureal, and an equally bumbling man-about-town, Hubert Connage, with the gentleman-crook who, despite his thievery, wins the hand of Hubert's sister. The script also included, among others, a pair of petulant servants, a pair of comical crooks, and a pair of adolescent girls who dance the turkey trot and sing Irving Berlin's 1911 hit, "Everybody's Doin' It Now." There were other improvements too. Fitzgerald had learned to introduce his expository material in a far less obvious manner than in his previous play (where much of it is included in Jack Darcy's opening monologue). In addition, the many reversals in plot here only added to the fun. His dialogue was greatly improved and he even attempted a number of dialects. Of course, there were still

[1] *New York Morning Telegraph*, November 12, 1922, Magazine Section, p. 3.

many flaws, possibly the most obvious being the many poor jokes. But in the main, the fifteen-year-old playwright had much to be proud of.

While writing the play, Fitzgerald had cast himself as the Shadow and Gustave Schurmeier as Hubert Connage. This is indicated in the tentative cast of characters in a partially torn leaf of his manuscript. Soon, however, changes occurred, including a switch in these two major parts. The title page and cast from Elizabeth Magoffin's transcription replaces Fitzgerald's list and precedes the first act here.

The Captured Shadow

By Francis Scott Fitzgerald

A Melodramatic-Comedy in Two Acts
Written for The Elizabethan Dramatic Club and
Presented on Friday evening, August 23, 1912
at Oak Hall
Under the direction of Elizabeth Magoffin.

Seven males Five females

Time of presentation—One hour

SYNOPSIS OF SCENES

Act I—*Drawing room of Mr. Connage, New York City.*
Act II—*The same.*
Time of action—*about 10:30 P. M.*

CAST OF CHARACTERS

HUBERT CONNAGE	Lawrence Boardman
THORTON HART DUDLEY, *alias* "*The Shadow*"	F. Scott Fitzgerald
MISS SAUNDERS, *housekeeper*	Dorothy Greene
MR. BEVERLY CONNAGE, *father of Hubert*	Paul Ballion
MRS. BEVERLY CONNAGE, *mother of Hubert*	Margaret Winchester
DOROTHY CONNAGE, *sister of Hubert*	Anne Winchester
HELEN MAYBURN, *friend of Dorothy*	Eleanor Alair
RABBIT SIMMONS (*Crooks*)	Theodore Parkhouse
CHINYMAN RUDD (*Crooks*)	James Porterfield
OFFICER MCGINNESS (*Detectives*) .	John L. Mitchell
OFFICER LEON DUREAL (*Detectives*) .	George Squires
EMMA KATE, *the maid*	Julia Dorr

The Captured Shadow

ACT I

(*Discovered: Emma Kate sitting asleep in the armchair.*)
(*Pause 10 seconds.*)

(*Voice outside heard singing "Silver Threads Among the Gold."*)
(*Enter Miss Saunders B. L. E.*) (*She puts on lights.*)
(*She crosses to the center of the stage, sees Emma Kate and folds her arms.*)

MISS S.: Well!

(*Pause 4 seconds.*)

MISS S.: Well!

(*Emma Kate stirs uneasily and rubs her eyes.*)

EMMA K.: (*Drowsily.*) Oh yes—yes mum.

MISS S.: (*Sternly.*) What on earth have you been doing?

EMMA K.: (*Sitting up.*) Asleepin', mum.

MISS S.: Sleeping, and in that chair. The best chair.

EMMA K.: Yes mum.

MISS S.: Do you realize that it is after ten o'clock?

EMMA K.: (*Getting up.*) Why Mrs. Connage tol' me as how I was to wait here for young Mr. Hubert. He's still out. An' as he wasn't come yet an' the chair was settin' there doin' nothin', I didn't think it'ud be no harm if I slept a bit, mum.

MISS S.: (*Shrugging her shoulders.*) So Mr. Hubert is still out, is he?

EMMA K.: Yes'm, Miss Saunders.

MISS S.: By the way, please brush out the chair.

EMMA K.: Why I ain't hurt the chair none.

MISS S.: (*Angrily.*) Please brush out the chair and no impudence.

EMMA K.: I wasn't meaning to be impudent. (*She starts to brush out the chair.*)

MISS S.: You may as well go to bed. I'll watch out for Mr. Hubert. I intend giving him a piece of my mind. The idea of the young man coming home intoxicated every night. (*Sits down at right.*)

EMMA K.: (*Turns towards her.*) Oh mum, he's adrinkin' awful. I've had to sit up for him almost every night an' I was awalkin' by Mrs. Connage's room today and I hears her say—(*Checks herself.*)

MISS S.: Aha! You were eavesdropping, were you? That's a nice trick. A nice trick, I must say.

EMMA K.: Honest to goodness, mum, I didn't mean to hear her talkin'.

MISS S.: That's a sly trick, Emma Kate, but I have detected you.

EMMA K.: Yes mum.

MISS S.: Well now. What did Mrs. Connage say?

EMMA K.: (*Surprised.*) Hmm?

MISS S.: What did she say?

EMMA K.: Why mum, a minute ago—

MISS S.: I have no personal interest in what Mrs. Connage was saying. I simply desire to know how much you have found out about the family secrets.

EMMA K.: I know most of the family secrets at that.

MISS S.: Eavesdroppers are certainly despicable creatures, heigh-ho —but I am waiting to hear what Mrs. Connage said.

EMMA K.: Between you and I, miss—

MISS S.: I and you, if you please.

EMMA K.: Cross your heart and hope to die if you tell?

MISS S.: How perfectly ridiculous. Of course I won't go through any such childish proceedings. I wish to find out what Mrs. Connage said.

EMMA K.: Well I was apassin' up the hall an' Mrs. Connage was atellin' to Mr. Connage 'at young Mr. Hubert had been in jail three days when his dad—when Mr. Connage thought he was in Atlantic City.

MISS S.: Preserve us! This is news, real news. Hmmm. (*Changing her tone suddenly.*) How perfectly awful for you to listen to all that. And did you hear anything else?

EMMA K.: An' Mr. Connage got awful mad. He swore some, too. Gee it was great! He kin swear better than the milkman. He said he'd turn Mr. Hubert out of the house and cut him off without a cent.

MISS S.: Dearie me! And what else did Mrs. Connage say? (*Dorothy outside.*)

DOROTHY: Miss Saunders.

MISS S.: You may go now. (*Emma Kate starts.*) But don't forget to brush out the chair. And no more of your mean sneaky eavesdropping tricks. (*Emma Kate starts to cry.*)

DOROTHY: (*Outside.*) Miss Saunders!

MISS S.: I am here, Miss Dorothy.

DOROTHY: (*At doorway with newspaper.*) Oh Miss Saunders, I've got the most fascinating newspaper article. (*Sees Emma Kate.*) Why, what's the matter here?

MISS S.: I found this girl monopolizing the best chair.

EMMA K.: (*Sniff, etc.*)

DOROTHY: Oh poor Emma Kate. Were you tired?

EMMA K.: Tired? No mum. No I'm never tired.

DOROTHY: She didn't hurt the chair, Miss S.

MISS S.: She sat in it. I asked her to retire.

EMMA K.: I'm goin'.

MISS S.: Have the kindness to hurry.

(*Exit Emma K.*)

DOROTHY: Miss Saunders, what's a sorehead?

MISS S.: Vulgar slang. And where did you hear that?

DOROTHY: Why Brother Hubert said you were an awful sorehead. (*Miss Saunders displeased.*)

MISS S.: (*Sees newspaper.*) Were you not forbidden to read newspapers?

DOROTHY: Oh yes, but I found the most romantic story.

MISS S.: Romantic bosh.

DOROTHY: It's about a burglar.

MISS S.: Horrors!

DOROTHY: Not an ordinary burglar.

MISS S.: What kind?

DOROTHY: He is called the Shadow. For two weeks the police have been after him but they can't catch him. He slips through their fingers. That's why they call him the Shadow. Oh they say he's so handsome.

MISS S.: Oh! (*Sighs.*)

DOROTHY: So accomplished!

MISS S.: Oh!! (*Sighs.*)

DOROTHY: And so wicked!

MISS S.: Oh! ! ! (*Startled.*)

DOROTHY: I like to imagine that he isn't really a burglar at all but only pretending to be one. Because he always sends back everything he steals with his compliments.

MISS S.: He does?

DOROTHY: Yes. And real burglars don't do that, do they?

MISS S.: Unfortunately they don't. But I am perfectly aware that the person who stole my watch last year was a real burglar.

DOROTHY: Really?

MISS S.: He might send that back and leave off the compliments. I'll give him the compliments if I catch him. That's the second Ingersoll I've lost in the space of ten years.

DOROTHY: Yes, it's terrible the way time flies. To change the subject, Helen Mayburn is coming over tonight to spend the night.

MISS S.: The poor girl that's going to marry your brother?

DOROTHY: Why Miss Saunders!

MISS S.: I think she is making a fool of herself to do it. And I have a right to my opinion. And I will tell Hubert so.

DOROTHY: Poor Hubert.

MISS S.: Poor Hubert, indeed!

(*Girl's voice outside singing—"Everybody's doin' it."*)

(*Enter Helen Mayburn. She sees Dorothy and stops in the doorway.*)

HELEN: Why hello Dorothy. What's the row about?

DOROTHY: Nothing at all.

MISS S.: Yes it is.

DOROTHY: (*To Miss Saunders.*) Don't you say a word.

MISS S.: Miss Mayburn, I feel it my duty to tell you that the man you are going to marry is a drunkard.

HELEN: Miss Saunders, he is not.

DOROTHY: Helen dear, don't listen to her.

MISS S.: Indeed! Let me tell you young ladies that you must behave quietly tonight.

DOROTHY: Oh we will.

HELEN: Of course.

MISS S.: And remember, no raids on the pantry. Last time you two were together you tried to steal some cake which I would have given you if you had asked me politely.

HELEN: Oh, but it was so much more fun to steal it.

MISS S.: And James thought you were burglars.

HELEN:
DOROTHY: } And we pushed him down stairs.

MISS S.: And he left the next morning. Well, we must have no more of that. Good evening, young ladies. (*Exit at L. B. E.*)

HELEN: What a most peculiar old lady.

DOROTHY: Very. She'll probably try to get you off in a corner and say all the mean things she can about Hubert.

HELEN: Well! When we have our little chat, I'll tell her what I think of her. Where is Hubert?

DOROTHY: Down town somewhere, I suppose. Come let us go upstairs.

HELEN: And Dorothy— we'll practice the turkey trot before the big mirror in the hall. Come on.

(*Exit the two.*)

(*Knocking outside.*)

(*Pause 5 seconds.*)

(*Knocking is repeated.*)

HUBERT: (*Outside.*) Ah, what in ze name of Pat is the matter now? Open ze darn old door. Can't a person enter his paternal residence wisout his key, 'specially when he's been so confounded unfortunate as to lose the old key? It's aggravating and antagonizing. Hello. Hello. (*Crash outside.*) There's a nice trick. Leave it unlocked all the time. Pick me up, boys. I'm not broken but only dented. Pick up those two teeth near the door. They may come in handy in the morning.

(*He appears tottering in the doorway.*)

HUBERT: Good evening. Why there's nobody home. (*Enter behind him Chinyman Rudd and Rabbit Simmons.*) Come in, gentlemen. Make yourself at home and sit down. (*Falls against Rudd, pushing him into chair. Then pushes Rabbit into chair. Tries to sit down.*) Pardon me, but could you give me a slight assistance? (*Rabbit pushes him into chair.*) Much obliged. My legs are a little stiff from walking.

RUDD: Say, is this where you hang out?

HUBERT: This is my domicile abode.

RABBIT: Your paternal hemorrhage?

RUDD: Heritage. You ain't got no edication.

RABBIT: Say, we've forgotten your name.

HUBERT: My name's Hubert Connage. Dad is Mr. Connage. Mother is Mrs. Connage. And my sister is Dorothy Connage. All the family, you see, have the same name. It's surprising to me, to say the least. I've often wondered what a remarkable coincidence it was that we all had the same name. There's Dad, one—he's really two but we'll count him one—and me, two. No, I'm one too. One, two, three, four.

RABBIT: Who the deuce are we for?

RUDD: Forty-seventh Street gang.

BOTH: Rah! Rah! Rah! (*Both whistle.*)

HUBERT: Hurray for you.

RUDD: Say, honest it's awful nice of you to pick us up on the streets and bring us back with you to spend the night, but what will your governor say?

HUBERT: Probably say "how-de-do."

RABBIT: I don't care if he only says it. What's worrying me is,—Has he got a dog?

HUBERT: No, there's no dog. There's a cat, tho'. Cutest little devil.

RABBIT: Divine, ain't it, Ching?

RUDD: Unsophisticating.

RABBIT: Oh chickering.

RUDD: Say, this reminds me of Charley's opium joint. All them there pictures and things.

RABBIT: (*Sees statue of Venus de Milo.*) Your mother swimmin'?

HUBERT: Mother? No. That's a good one. That's Venus de Milo.

RUDD: Pity you broke it. How did it bust?

RABBIT: Some one kicked it on the impulse of the moment.

HUBERT: I'm going to introduce you to Dad and tell him you're my friends and are going to spend the night with me.

RABBIT: The likes of us ain't for here. We both look like we been shot at an' missed. We don't move in the same circles.

HUBERT: I don't know about circles but I have lately been moving in all sorts of curves.

RUDD: We're—we're—a couple of crooks.

HUBERT: That's a good job. Are you married?

RABBIT: No, I got these scratches from a cat.

HUBERT: What are your names?

RUDD: On the island he's 96 and I'm 108.

RABBIT: In social life he's Chinyman Rudd and I'm Rabbit Simmons.

HUBERT: Rabbit, I had a rabbit once. Pretty little things, aren't they? This rabbit was an awful crook. He stole more lettuce. So you're burglars. What do you steal, bases?

RABBIT: We've been working for a fellow called the Shadow. He's a kind of a gentleman burglar. He goes around in a dress suit and robs houses. We spy around for him, see when the family is going to be at home, find out about valuables and he pays us five hundred dollars a week apiece.

HUBERT: Who the dickens is the Shadow?

RUDD: His real name's Thorton Hart. Nobody knows nothing about him. He acts just like a gentleman. He came about two weeks ago and he's about as nervy as they make 'em. They can't catch him. He slips through the cops every time.

HUBERT: A shadow, hey? Well I'll bet the old Shadow won't have time for reflection if some good detectives get after him. Ever read Sherlock Holmes, Mr. Bunny?

RABBIT: Rabbit. No. Ever read Nick Carter?

HUBERT: Never. Say, I don't want to see the poor old Shadow shackled. I hope the police don't get him.

RUDD: He's got on a job tonight. He says it's a big one but he won't tell us about it.

HUBERT: Success to him. Come, we'll drink to him. (*He fills up three glasses.*) To the Shadow! May he never have the great misfortune to be a captured Shadow.

ALL: To the Shadow! (*All drink.*)

HUBERT: Well, now I'll procure you fellows some clothes. Why the way you're dressed is a disgrace. I thought all crooks were rich. I'll find you some good clothes. You make yourself at home and help yourself. (*Exit.*)

RABBIT: Well here's our chance. Pile in a bagful of that silverware and beat it quick.

RUDD: Aw say, nix.

RABBIT: Why not?

RUDD: When the guy meets us on the street, then brings us home and tells us he's going to have us here to spend the night, we oughtn't to rush off with his silver. H'ain't you got no manners?

RABBIT: Just look. What couldn't we do with this and this. Hold me back, please.

RUDD: I got enough to do holding myself.

BOTH: Ohh. (*Sighing.*)

(*Enter Hubert with clothes.*)

HUBERT: Now here's some clothes. You go in there and put 'em on. Try to look respectable and I'll introduce you to Dad.

RUDD: What does your dad weigh?

RABBIT: How's his punch?

HUBERT: Don't know, but his whiskey's darn good.

RUDD: Say, are these ours for keeps?
HUBERT: Sure.
RABBIT: Well I'll leave my things here in exchange. They ain't much to look at but they're valuable as relics. It would grieve me if they were thrown away.
HUBERT: Don't worry. I'll put 'em in a glass case.
RABBIT: Say, this is awful good of you even if you are tight.
HUBERT: Oh that's all right, Mr. Hare.
RABBIT: Rabbit, Rabbit.
HUBERT: Rabies!
RABBIT: Rabbit.
HUBERT: Where?
RABBIT: Naw, Rabbit is my name.
HUBERT: Oh! I couldn't imagine what you were talking about. Ha-Ha— (*Laughs.*)
RABBIT: Where do we change?
HUBERT: In there. Oh. (*Something occurs to him.*) (*Laughs.*) I've got the greatest scheme. Aldermen.
RUDD: Where?
HUBERT: You! (*Still convulsed with laughter.*)
RABBIT: He's dippy.
RUDD: Poor guy.
HUBERT: Now don't you see? I'll introduce you as aldermen from the Seventh Ward.
RUDD: (*Doubtfully.*) Hm!
RABBIT: Crooked politics.
RUDD: Say, do we look like aldermen?
HUBERT: Exactly, and it'll be a capital joke on Dad.
RABBIT: No alderman has got anything on me. Clarence, pass the sherry.
RUDD: The skenatcho sauce, please.
HUBERT: Now remember, you're aldermen from the S-s-t Ward.
RABBIT: The what?
HUBERT: The Whist Ward.
RUDD: Try and whistle it.
RABBIT: S-t.
HUBERT: Thixth. There it is. Thixth Ward.
RUDD: Not the Sixth. There's an awful lot of roughnecks in the Sixth Ward.
RABBIT: Mercy me. How perfectly fumigating.

HUBERT: Now you fellows come along and jump into these duds and then you can reform Tammany Hall.

(Exit Hubert and Rudd.)

(Rabbit sneaks over and fills a glass full of whiskey.)

(A head is poked cautiously in the back door. The Shadow is seen. He sees Rabbit and starts. He sneaks up to the table, seizes a book and throws it at Rabbit's feet. Rabbit jumps.)

RABBIT: The Shadow.

SHADOW: Well?

RABBIT: What are you doing here?

SHADOW: That's just what I was going to ask you.

RABBIT: I am here with a special invitation.

SHADOW: I am here with no invitation at all. In fact I intend to rob this house.

RABBIT: So this is the job you wouldn't tell us about.

SHADOW: Exactly. Now what are you doing here?

RABBIT: I am thinking of going into politics.

SHADOW: Rabbit!

RABBIT: I've got a job as an alderman. Sixth Ward.

SHADOW: Alderman?

RABBIT: That's straight goods. I've always been fond of politics and now, why I've got some prominent capitalists backing me and— *(Shrugs his shoulders.)* The father of my chief backer owns this house and I'm spending the night with him.

SHADOW: Is he crazy?

RABBIT: No.

SHADOW: Drunk?

RABBIT: How the deuce did you know?

SHADOW: Why *(laughs)* I thought he might be.

RABBIT: You're tryin' to kid me now. I'd really make a good alderman, tho'. I never was cut out for a crook. I was born for something better. Sometimes I get thinking that I ought to been a minister. Gosh! You ought to see me kiss a baby.

SHADOW: Don't take advantage of a child, Rabbit. The poor things can't defend themselves.

RABBIT: Hm?

SHADOW: I have no doubt you're a pious youth and will make a simply great alderman and a model politician.

RABBIT: Well, how about you? You're not so bad as you try to pretend to be. I don't think you're no crook at all. Why do you pack up all the stuff you steal and send it back to the people you steal it from with "the compliments of the Shadow" on a little card? I seen you sendin' back the stuff you steal. You act as if you were doing it for fun.

SHADOW: Maybe I am, Rabbit, maybe I am.

RABBIT: If you're trying the crook business simply to find out what it's like or to get fun out of it, why, you'd better cut it out. It doesn't pay.

SHADOW: Enough of this. I intend to do a little work tonight and see what I can pick up around the place. I must get familiar with the house and introduce myself to the inhabitants. Let me see. "House owned by Mr. Connage, married. Two children, Hubert and Dorothy, twenty-two and eighteen respectively, and Miss Saunders, housekeeper." Hubert must have been the one you say you are acquainted with.

RABBIT: Yes, we are on quite intimate terms.

SHADOW: I'll look him up. In the meanwhile, of course, you'll say nothing to any one about my being in the house.

RABBIT: Mum as a mouse.

SHADOW: And now for inspection. (*Exit the Shadow.*)

(*Enter Rudd in a light check suit smoking black cigar.*)

RABBIT: Well look at the duds.

RUDD: A little tasty class. They belong to the butler. Mr. Connage didn't have any sporty enough for me.

(*Voice outside.*)

MRS. CONNAGE: Beverly, oh Beverly.

RABBIT: Beat it quick.

RUDD: Stand your ground. It's the lady of the house.

RABBIT: Oh. Oh. (*Shivering.*)

MRS. C.: (*Coming in.*) Ah, callers. (*To the crooks.*) Good evening, gentlemen.

RUDD: Evenin'.

RABBIT: Howdy.

MRS. C.: Have you called to see Mr. Connage?

RUDD: Well not exactly.

MRS. C.: Or Miss Connage?

RUDD: Not minutely.

MRS. C.: Have you called to see me?

RABBIT: Not precisely.

RUDD: The truth is we're aldermen from the Sixth Ward.

RABBIT: Personal friends of your son.

RUDD: What do they call you?

MRS. C.: I am Mrs. Connage. Well I'm afraid my son isn't home yet.

RABBIT: Oh we just left him.

MRS. C.: Is he in the house?

RUDD: (*Aside to Rabbit.*) Lie to her. If she finds him drunk we'll get kicked out.

MRS. C.: Where is he?

RABBIT: Why he's pie-eyed.

(*Rudd cautions him.*)

RUDD: Sh-Sh.

MRS. C.: My son been having trouble with his eyes?

RUDD: He was half shot.

MRS. C.: (*Screams.*) Shot in the eye? Who shot him?

RABBIT: Well, when a guy gets half shot he usually does it himself.

RUDD: That's so.

MRS. C.: He shot himself?

RUDD:
RABBIT: } He did.

RABBIT: (*Aside.*) A pretty mess.

MRS. C.: My heavens. This is terrible. Where is he?

RUDD: Why he's here— I mean he's—a—

RABBIT: Down town in a room of my boarding house.

(*Mrs. Connage faints in the arms of Rabbit.*)

RABBIT: Get some water quick.

RUDD: There ain't none. Will whiskey do?

RABBIT: Anything.

(*They give her whiskey. She revives.*)

MRS. C.: I must go to him at once. Wait for me. I'll get my wraps.

(*Exit Mrs. Connage.*)

RUDD: Well you did it.

RABBIT: You mean you did it.

RUDD: Whoever did it, between us, we're in a pretty hole.

RABBIT: Well let's clear out o' here fore she comes down.

(*They look out entrances.*)

RUDD: Coast's clear.

(*They tiptoe out.*)

(*Enter Mr. Connage followed by Miss Saunders.*)

MISS S.: But Mr. Connage.

MR. C.: No buts. My daughter informs me that you have been extracting bits of information from the servants and this alone would make me discharge you. But the idea of your throwing all my cigars out the window because you thought they were cartridges, that is too much!

MISS S.: But I did think they were cartridges. They smelt like it.

MR. C.: No matter. I asked you to leave in the morning and leave you shall. I am a man of my word.

MISS S.: But this is a serious step. Think. I have been with you so long and served you so well.

MR. C.: If you are here by tomorrow I will have you forcibly removed.

MISS S.: Such is my lot to be derided and misunderstood. Such is my fate.

MR. C.: Oh you still here?

MISS S.: Dear Mr. Connage—

MR. C.: Ohh!

(*Violent ringings of the doorbell, shouts, hammering at door.*)

EMMA K.: (*Coming in at back.*) Oh Mr. Connage, there are a lot of policemen at the gate all yelling that there's a thief in the house. They're breaking in.

MR. C.: A thief in my house?

MISS S.: Where, where?

EMMA K.: Oh what shall we do?

MISS S.: They've broken in.

EMMA K.: Here they come.

MR. C.: This is an outrage.

(*Tramping in the hall. Enter a policeman.*)

McGINNESS: Stop. I'll enter. Sir, there's a burglar in the house. We saw him enter.

MR. C.: Impossible!

McGINNESS: Nevertheless, it's so.

EMMA K.: There is no burglar.

MISS S.: There may be.

McGINNESS: If you are concealing him— Leon!

(*Enter Leon Dureal.*)

LEON: Oui, oui, monsieur.

McGINNESS: Guard the stairs! Marshal the inmates. Search the house. We have reason to believe that the thief is none other than the famous Shadow himself.

MISS S.: The Shadow?

MR. C.: In my house?

MISS S.: Terrible!

EMMA K.: Awful!

VOICES OUTSIDE: Catch the thief. After him. Catch the Shadow. Nab the crook.

(*Enter the girls.*)

DOROTHY: What is the matter?

MR. C.: These men say there's a burglar in the house.

LEON: Up ze stairs, men. I will lead and for ze honor of ze gen d'armes of France. Forward brave comrades.

MCGINNESS: Up the stairs.

MR. C.: One hundred dollars to the one that catches him.

MISS S.: One hundred dollars!

ALL: The Shadow! After him! Down with the thief! Capture the burglar! A cool hundred! Nab the reward! (*Etc.*)

(*All talking at once, they rush out of the room. Enter the Shadow around the door at left.*)

SHADOW: Well here's a pretty fix, to say the least. Policemen all around the house. Policemen in it and all looking for me. They probably saw me coming in. How to get out is what's worrying me.

(*Enter Hubert from right.*)

HUBERT: What's all this row about? Why, what do you want here?

SHADOW: Are you Mr. Hubert Connage?

HUBERT: Yes, Mr.—Mr.—?

SHADOW: Johnston. I called to see about the furnace.

HUBERT: Why our furnace is all right. You've got the wrong house. (*Edges him toward door.*)

SHADOW: The truth is, I called to see your father. Is he in?

HUBERT: He is.

SHADOW: But you will do just as well. Let me see. What day of the month is this?

HUBERT: The twenty-second, I think. I never keep track after twelve o'clock.

SHADOW: Well, to proceed to business. This is the twelfth.

HUBERT: No, I said I never keep track after twenty-two—I mean twelve o'clock.

SHADOW: Well twenty-two years ago next April—May—

HUBERT: Hm!

SHADOW: Why, what's the matter?

HUBERT: You been drinking too?

SHADOW: No, certainly not. That's the new fashioned way. Instead of saying "April and May," you say "April-May." Like, for instance, "April, maybe June, but always March."

HUBERT: Yes. What?

SHADOW: You understand, I hope.

HUBERT: Clear as mud.

SHADOW: Listen. As I said, twenty years ago—

HUBERT: You said ten.

SHADOW: Did I? Split the difference and call it fifteen. Add six makes twenty-one; add seven and divide by two—I have fourteen, what have you?

HUBERT: Go on. I want to see how much a fellow sees and hears when he's drunk or how much he thinks he hears. Do you think you can persuade me I'm talking to you? You can't. I'm in bed sleeping as comfortable— (*Turns but falls out of chair.*) Why in the dickens didn't you try and persuade me I wasn't?

SHADOW: Because of Irving Berlin. Do you realize that he made thirty thousand on "Alexander's Ragtime Band"?

HUBERT: Look here—this is gone far enough. I've made aldermen and been to sleep tonight but I'm awake now and I never listened to such a lot of nonsense as you've been talking. What in the devil are you doing in the house anyways?

VOICE OUTSIDE: After him. Catch the Shadow! Shackle the thief!

HUBERT: The Shadow, why here? What are *you* doing here? The Shadow. The Shadow. Are you the Shadow? Well, I'll be—

SHADOW: Surprised.

HUBERT: I guess they've got you now, Mr. Shadow, or whatever they call you. When I yell, as I'm going to, it's Sing Sing for you.

SHADOW: But you won't yell.

HUBERT: I won't?

SHADOW: You won't.

HUBERT: And why not?

SHADOW: Because I say so.

HUBERT: We'll see. Fa—!

SHADOW: Stop. Hand up!

HUBERT: (*Puts hand up.*)

SHADOW: Hand down. I have no gun.

HUBERT: I'm a fool. Fath—!

SHADOW: One more word and your fiancée, Miss—Miss—(*looks at paper*) Miss Helen Mayburn, will know where you were those three days last week. And it wasn't Atlantic City.

HUBERT: Good heavens! What do you want?

SHADOW: I intend robbing this house if there is anything here that interests me.

HUBERT: What do you want of me?

SHADOW: Your absolute silence concerning me, nothing else.

HUBERT: Well you shall have it since you know so much. And how did you know I was in prison three days last week?

SHADOW: Simply enough. I was the policeman who arrested you. I saw you were drunk, saw you break in an old man's derby, and I thought I'd give you a vacation.

HUBERT: You were that ugly cop with the long beard?

SHADOW: A rather doubtful compliment but I was he or he was I. Anyways, the problem now is this. They saw me enter this house. Some of them are in it. Some are out of it. I've got to get out.

HUBERT: Well I hope they catch you.

SHADOW: Remember, not a word from you.

HUBERT: They'll catch you anyways.

SHADOW: They can't.

HUBERT: Can't?

SHADOW: Look here—when you were little did you ever chase a reflection?

HUBERT: Yes, but never caught it.

SHADOW: Of course not. Not only because you couldn't catch it but because it was an impossibility. Did you ever hear of a captured shadow?

HUBERT: No.

SHADOW: Of course not. There's no such thing. It's contrary to science. Now, I'm a shadow. So there you are.

HUBERT: You will be a captured Shadow before four hours.

SHADOW: Think as you please. I shall permit you to retire now. Good evening.

HUBERT: What?

SHADOW: You may go.

HUBERT: This is my house.

SHADOW: You may go.

HUBERT: Oh very well. (*Exit.*)

(*Enter Miss S.*)

MISS S.: Why, who are you?

SHADOW: Don't be alarmed.

MISS S.: My nerves are in a turmoil. They say there is a thief in the house.

SHADOW: There is but I'll get him. I am a detective, my dear lady.

MISS S.: So you're a detective, are you?

SHADOW: I am.

MISS S.: A real detective?

SHADOW: What do I look like? Papier maché?

MISS S.: And do you need assistance?

SHADOW: Assistance? Ah, I have just the thing. Sh!

MISS S.: Oh, if I could help you find this burglar, Mr. Connage might take me back in his employ.

SHADOW: Listen. I am hunting for the Shadow. I should like your assistance in a piece of work that requires careful handling. Now take heed. The real burglar is no other than Mr. Connage himself. He has been deceiving people for years but at last I'm onto him.

MISS S.: How perfectly awful. Still, I had long suspected.

SHADOW: Now the next person who enters this room I want you to stop and hold here till I come. Have you a revolver?

MISS S.: I'll get one. (*Takes revolver from case on wall.*)

SHADOW: Now remember, no matter who the person is. Hold him or her up until I come, for I have reason to suspect that it will be Mr. Connage's assistant. Remember, the police do not treat courageous work lightly. You will probably be rewarded and— How would you like a position on the women's detective bureau?

MISS S.: Magnificent!

SHADOW: You will obtain it. Now crawl under this table. Don't fire under any conditions and remember that "wait" and "hope" are the passwords.

MISS S.: Wait and hope. I will remember.

(*Exit Shadow. She crawls under table.*)

(*Enter Mrs. Connage in coat and shawl.*)

MRS. C.: Gentlemen, I am ready to see my son. Why they're gone. Where on earth—

MISS S.: (*Under table.*) Halt. Not another step.

MRS. C.: What—what!

MISS S.: I have you covered.

MRS. C.: Oh who are you?

MISS S.: One of the foremost members of the women's secret service.
MRS. C.: It's Miss Saunders.
MISS S.: You have been found out.
MRS. C.: The woman is crazy!
MISS S.: Put up your hands.
MRS. C.: She is in league with some robbers.
MISS S.: The signs of guilt are written all over your face.
MRS. C.: Miss Saunders, release me at once. My son is lying half shot in a boarding house and I must go to him.
MISS S.: What language. Half shot indeed!
MRS. C.: Will you kindly explain this?
MISS S.: No explanation is necessary. (*Comes out from table.*) I have you where I want you. My friend the detective will soon arrive.
MRS. C.: But—
MISS S.: No explanations. I know all.
MRS. C.: All what?
MISS S.: All about your husband.
MRS. C.: (*Aside.*) Heavens! Can he have been up to something?
MISS S.: He has indeed. And you know only too well. You are his accomplice.
MRS. C.: His accomplice? Me?
MISS S.: You.

(*Enter Mr. Connage from back.*)

MRS. C.: Beverly!
MR. C.: Why, what's all this about? A pistol!
MISS S.: Put up your hands.
MR. C.: What?
MRS. C.: She says you're a criminal.
MR. C.: What in the devil is the matter?
MRS. C.: And I've just received word that our son is shot.
MR. C.: Shot? I just saw him. (*To Miss S.*) Did you shoot him?
MISS S.: Everything you say will be used against you.
MR. C.: This is preposterous.
MRS. C.: She must be in league with robbers.
MISS S.: You rascal, you!
MR. C.: (*To his wife.*) Have you been up to something?

(*Voices outside.*)

DUREAL: We have zem.

McGinness: Bring them in here.

(Enter the policemen, each holding either Rabbit or Rudd, followed by Emma Kate.)

McGinness: We found them trying to sneak out of the back window. They have stolen these clothes.

Dureal: We have did ze duty.

McGinness: But what's all this?

Mr. C.: Arrest this woman. *(Pointing to Miss Saunders.)*

Miss S.: Arrest this man. *(Pointing to Mr. Connage.)*

McGinness: But we have the crooks.

Miss S.: Pardon me but I have them.

Mrs. C.: But this woman is evidently a thief herself.

Dureal: Four crooks or five. Ah, this is a situation.

McGinness: Who— Who— What shall I do?

Dureal: These are the men.

Mr. C.: }
Mrs. C.: } This is the woman.

Miss S.: Apprehend this couple.

McGinness: But which one shall I arrest?

Dureal: Arrest all of zem.

(Enter Hubert followed by girls.)

Dorothy: Papa! Mama!

Mrs. C.: My son, restored!

Helen: Miss Saunders!

Hubert: Rabbit and Chinyman!

Rabbit: Well?

McGinness: What shall I do? They each accuse somebody else.

Hubert: These are my friends. I'll vouch for 'em.

Dorothy: This is my father and mother.

Dureal: Ze case grows complicated.

Rabbit: Arrest the old lady with the shotgun.

Hubert: You're looking for the Shadow? There ain't five Shadows.

(Enter the Shadow.)

Shadow: No, there are not. But the Shadow is here.

Dureal: Shall I arrest this fellow too?

Miss S.: My friend the detective.

Shadow: I'm Johnston from the central office.

McGinness: Well, see if you can unravel this.

Shadow: I think I can. The Shadow is in this room.

(All start.)

MCGINNESS: Where? Where?

SHADOW: Look! The crook will be known in two minutes. Listen! Some one in this room is posing for some one else, but in reality is the Shadow.

ALL: The Shadow?

SHADOW: The most daring crook in New York. He is one who has for years been leading a double life. Officer. Arrest Hubert Connage, alias the Shadow.

ALL: Hubert Connage?

HUBERT: It's a lie!!

MRS. C.: My son.

(*Hubert starts up. They grab him. All are startled and talk. Mrs. Connage faints and the Shadow lights a cigarette.*)

(*Curtain.*)

ACT II

(*Thirty minutes later. Scene the same. Mr. Connage is seated at left. McGinness is standing at right and Hubert is gagged and tied to chair between them. Dureal is standing to the right of McGinness.*)

MR. C.: So now I hope you are convinced that my son is no burglar and no Shadow and that this is all a foolish mistake.

MCGINNESS: Well I guess it's pretty certain that you ought to know your own son, but you'll admit it looked mighty suspicious when that detective fellow stood out here and called him the Shadow.

DUREAL: Mais ou est-t-il. Le detective qui a lui denoncé.

MCGINNESS: Yes, yes. Speak sensibly.

DUREAL: That detective. Where has he disappeared?

MCGINNESS: He said he was going to call up the police station.

MR. C.: But that was a half an hour ago.

MCGINNESS: Well he hasn't come back.

MR. C.: Had you ever seen him before?

MCGINNESS: Never. He said he'd just joined the force.

MR. C.: I half believe he wasn't a detective at all.

MCGINNESS: Well he couldn't have gone far. There's a guard of policemen around the house.

DUREAL: I knew, I knew continually, what ch'u call it, all ze time. I—ze brain, oui, moi.

McGinness: Your mouth is overcrowded with talk. Now spill one word at a time and you'll be understood.

Dureal: I knew all the time.

McGinness: And you didn't tell us? Why you mean little thing. He was a gent dee harm in France.

Dureal: Oui j'etais un gen d'arme en Paris. I nevaire before fail. That we have not caught him is due to this pig.

McGinness: Here, here, frogslegs— No names.

Dureal: Frogslegs?

Mr. C.: Gentlemen. It is not too late to catch this burglar or bogus detective. There is still a guard of policemen around the house, so he must be in the house.

Hubert: (*Gagged.*) Mmmmm—mmm—mm—mmmm.

Mr. C.: My son evidently wants to be released.

McGinness: To be sure. I forgot.

(*Unties him.*)

Hubert: Mmm— Ah. Oh my mouth. (*Tries to stretch it.*) Of all the ivory-headed policemen. To let that fellow get away from almost under your nose.

Dureal: What fellow?

Hubert: That fake detective. Why he was the Shadow himself.

McGinness:
Mr. C.:
Dureal: } He was the Shadow?

Hubert: Of course he was. If I hadn't been a little intoxicated I wouldn't have let him bluff me about keeping mum.

McGinness: You knew who he was all the time?

Hubert: Sure I did but he threatened to blab something he knew about me if I gave him away, but now he's played me such a dirty trick and got my mouth so sore that I am going to catch that fellow if he tells about me all over town.

Mr. C.: Mr. McGinness has stationed men all around the house, so he couldn't have gotten away.

Dureal: Well, after him.

McGinness: Right-o.

Mr. C.: Come, we will search the house.

(*Exit McGinness, Dureal, Mr. Connage.*)

(*Enter Mrs. Connage.*)

Mrs. C.: Hubert, Hubert, my poor boy. So they released you. First some aldermen told me that you had been shot.

HUBERT: Aldermen? I don't remember any alderman. Oh yes, I have a dim recollection of picking up two men on the street and bringing them home and why—yes—why I promised I'd make them aldermen or something of the sort.

MRS. C.: But my son, they said you had been shot in the eye and your eye looks all right. Where were you shot?

HUBERT: In the excitement.

(*Enter Helen.*)

HELEN: Oh excuse me. There has been so much excitement that I don't know where I'm going.

HUBERT: Why Helen, just in time. Mother, Helen and I are—are— Oh why don't you tell her?

HELEN: We're—we're— Why don't you?

HUBERT: Engaged.

HELEN: To be married.

MRS. C.: Engaged? Why, why, how startling! But Helen, you dear girl, I haven't the heart to blame you. You must tell me all about it in the morning. Come, it is getting late.

HELEN: Here Hubert. Something I got for you down town today. (*Hands him paper.*) Sign it.

HUBERT: What is it?

HELEN: Why it's a pledge.

(*Exit Helen and Mrs. C.*)

HUBERT: Well I'll be darned. (*Starts to throw it away, then examines it, then signs it and throws it on the table.*)

(*Enter Rudd and Rabbit.*)

HUBERT: Ah, good morning Mr.—Mr.—

RABBIT: You ain't forgotten us, have you?

HUBERT: Oh are you the fellows I brought home to spend the night with me?

RABBIT: We're the ones. And say, you haven't forgotten about aldermen?

HUBERT: Hey, did I say I'd make you aldermen? What a fool I was!

RABBIT: Oh I don't know about that.

HUBERT: I tell you. I'll consider the matter at least. You may spend the night as my guest.

RABBIT: But— But— But—

RUDD: You talk like a goat.

HUBERT: Where did you get that suit? It's enough to wake any one up in the morning.

RUDD: Think so? You gave it to me.

HUBERT: You mean that I ever had a suit like that?

RUDD: You said I could take it out of the butler's clothes press.

RABBIT: It looks cheap.

RUDD: Cheap? Why it's all covered with big checks.

HUBERT: And here is a retaining fee and a happy rest to you both and—sh—sh—keep it dark about our political prospects. (*Exit Hubert.*)

RABBIT: I'm going to insure my money so if I spend it I will have it anyways.

RUDD: Come, we'll go to bed. Say, is the Shadow still in the house? Wasn't it slick when he told the cops that Hubert was the Shadow?

RABBIT: I guess they're onto him now. Well let's hope he gets out of the house safely. We know how it is.

(*Exit both of them.*)

(*Enter the Shadow.*)

SHADOW: Well I'm in for it. I'm as good as caught. The Shadow caught, captured. After baffling the New York police for two weeks, to be caught like an ordinary second story man. Still, they can't do much to me. I can prove that I have sent back every bit of stuff that I stole. But to be captured and by such ivory heads as this McGinness. Still, I must not give up. I'm not caught yet, not by a long shot. There is still a chance. One chance in a hundred, but a chance all the same.

(*Enter Dorothy.*)

DOROTHY: Why it's the detective. How do you do, sir. Sir, tell me. Why did you accuse my brother? Will you release him?

SHADOW: Release him? Why, of course, if you wish.

DOROTHY: I didn't know detectives were so obliging. But tell me. Is the Shadow in this house? And who is the Shadow?

SHADOW: I'm afraid it would be imprudent to tell you. You might put him on his guard.

DOROTHY: Is he as romantic looking as the newspapers say?

SHADOW: I should say not. He is an undersized, bullet-headed fellow. As ugly as I have ever seen, Miss Connage.

DOROTHY: Well then, why did you take my brother for him?

SHADOW: Why—oh yes—why yes—of course— Why that's the question. Ha-ha. Well let me see. It's a long story and my time for business is short. Listen. He is in this house and I must catch him.

DOROTHY: I wish you success, Mr.—Mr.—

SHADOW: Johnston.

DOROTHY: Mr. Johnston. But I am disappointed that the Shadow was not handsome for I had intended to fall in love with him.

SHADOW: You had? Poor fellow that he doesn't know it. He would jump at the chance but you would have no use for a fellow like that.

DOROTHY: You never can tell. Good night, Mr. Johnston, and good luck.

(*She goes out. He shakes his head sadly and then goes out.*)

(*Enter from opposite sides Rabbit and Miss Saunders.*)

MISS S.: What a noble looking being!

RABBIT: Discovered.

MISS S.: Ah, 'tis the politician. I thought I heard a noise in the library.

RABBIT: It must have been only the history repeating itself.

MISS S.: And how are you, dear sir?

RABBIT: I'm so thin from all this excitement that my shadow would puncture a bicycle tire.

MISS S.: Quite clever. You know I'm not as old as I look.

RABBIT: You couldn't be and live.

MISS S.: He is eccentric. But will you not have a chocolate drop, sir? "Sweets to the sweet," you know.

RABBIT: Have some of these. (*Passes crackers.*) Crackers to the cracked, you know.

MISS S.: Sir, I'll have you know I'll not be openly derided. Emma Kate. Show this man the door.

(*Emma Kate comes in.*)

EMMA K.: And no mum.

MISS S.: What?

EMMA K.: You was discharged this evenin'. I he'r Mr. Connage atellin' you.

MISS S.: Entirely utterly crushed! I shall pray, and let me tell you my prayers will be heard, that this house will be swallowed by an earthquake— There! (*Exit.*)

RABBIT: And it's good riddance to bad rubbish. Emma Kate, do you suppose that in the kitchen there is a little chicken and a bottle of beer ready to be eaten up?

EMMA K.: There might be.

RABBIT: Come along then.

(*Exeunt the two.*)

(*Enter the Shadow followed by Dureal whom he does not see.*)

SHADOW: Policemen at the front door, policemen at the back door, policemen at the side door and policemen at every window. How shall I get out? Let me see. Oh! the telephone.

DUREAL: Non, monsier. You are my prisoner.

SHADOW: Me your prisoner? You mean your guest.

DUREAL: I, Dureal, have captured you. Hands up.

SHADOW: Oh, is your name Dureal, the famous Dureal?

DUREAL: What, you know me? (*He is pleased.*)

SHADOW: Who has not heard of you—the cleverest gen d'arme in Paris, the handsomest and most efficient man on the New York police force.

DUREAL: Monsieur. But are you not the Shadow?

SHADOW: Yes I am, and you unaided have captured me. But it is no disgrace to be captured by you. It is rather an honor.

DUREAL: Monsuer.

SHADOW: Monsieur.

DUREAL: You are too polite.

SHADOW: One could never equal a Frenchman in politeness. But forgive me. You will sit down?

DUREAL: With pleasure.

SHADOW: But there is one thing I never could understand about the French police. Could you explain it? I hear they lock all the criminals in one large room. Now what's to prevent them from breaking out?

DUREAL: But they don't. They lock the prisoners in cells.

SHADOW: Surprising. Well now. How big are these cells? As big as these closets? (*Opens closet door.*)

DUREAL: Oh yes.

SHADOW: But now a man of your size couldn't get in this closet.

DUREAL: Why certainly. Here. I will go in—

(*Walks into closet. Shadow slams and locks door.*)

SHADOW: And you'll stay there too. Monsieur Monsieur. (*Laughs.*)

(*Dureal stamps and pounds.*)

SHADOW: And it's always safer to work in the dark. (*Extinguishes lights and lights candle on table.*)

(*Enter McGinness. He gives a cry of satisfaction and covers Shadow with a revolver. Shadow grabs up magazine and throws it so that it knocks revolver from policeman's hand. He jumps over chair and grapples with policeman.*)

McGINNESS: Curse you, curse you.

SHADOW: Give up or I'll break your arm.

(*Enter Hubert followed by his father. He snatches up the candle and points revolver at Shadow.*)

HUBERT: Now we've got you, Mr. Shadow, or whatever you call yourself.

(*Enter Dorothy, Helen, Miss S., Mrs. C., Emma K., and crooks.*)

SHADOW: Yes, you've got me at last. I'm caught.

HUBERT: I thought there was no such thing as a captured Shadow.

DOROTHY: So you're a burglar?

SHADOW: A burglar. Me— Yes.

McGINNESS: Well it was no cinch, and for two weeks you've led us a hard chase.

SHADOW: I guess the game is up. But you know I'm not yet in the lockup. But I'd better make a clean sweep of it. My accomplice is in that closet.

McGINNESS: Bosh and nonsense! It's one of his tricks.

SHADOW: Will some one listen to me?

DOROTHY: I will listen to you.

SHADOW: Then listen. In that closet is locked some one who will be useful to you.

(*Poundings.*)

But he is desperate. So you must bind him directly. You take that shawl and throw it over his head. Here is the key. Ready. Unlock it.

(*McGinness unlocks door. Dureal comes out. They throw shawl over head, not recognizing him. Shadow steps behind screen in the excitement. Dureal sputters and fumes.*)

DUREAL: Fools. Fools. Where is he?

McGINNESS: (*Looking around.*) Gone!

ALL: Where?

HUBERT: After him!

DUREAL: Oh me, oh my!

(*Exit all.*)

(*Shadow comes quickly from behind screen and steps to telephone.*)

(*Enter Dorothy.*)

DOROTHY: Well?

SHADOW: Well? (*Takes up phone.*)

DOROTHY: Put down that phone.

SHADOW: The phone? (*Takes down receiver.*)

DOROTHY: Yes, or—

SHADOW: Nonsense. Hello— Hello. Oh here they are.

DOROTHY: If you say one word over that phone, I'll shoot.

SHADOW: You will? Very well. Central, give me the Forty-fourth Street police station. All right. Why don't you fire?

DOROTHY: I—I can't.

SHADOW: And why not?

DOROTHY: I don't know.

SHADOW: Hello— Is this the Forty-fourth Street police station? Well this is Officer McGinness. I am at the Connages' house on Fifty-second Street. Immediately withdraw the guard from around the house. We've caught the Shadow at last. Thank you. Good evening. And please hurry. (*Bangs down receiver.*)

DOROTHY: If I wished I could summon the police or counteract that telephone message.

SHADOW: Why don't you scream? I won't stop you.

DOROTHY: Because I'm not going to. I am going to let you get out of here. Listen—tell me the truth. Who are you? You don't seem like a burglar. And is it true that you send back everything you steal?

SHADOW: People seem to be onto me. Yes, I guess it is true.

DOROTHY: Are you a real thief then?

SHADOW: Why of course.

DOROTHY: I wished you weren't.

SHADOW: You wish I wasn't?

DOROTHY: I—I—would like to have known you better. But as it is, it is out of the question.

SHADOW: Yes, it's out, out of the question. For I am only a burglar. Not fit to look at you.

DOROTHY: But why— Why are you a burglar?

SHADOW: Because I was born to it, I suppose.

DOROTHY: Born to it? You were not born to it. You are a gentleman.

SHADOW: Thank you, miss. Well, you are right in a way. By entering houses by stealth I've forfeited all claims to the name of gentleman, but I've never kept a thing I've taken and I'm glad you think I am. But as I am for the present a burglar, it is better we should not meet again. (*At window.*) I see the guard has been withdrawn. Good night, Miss Connage. Were I not a burglar, I might hope to know you better. But— (*Opens door.*) (*Clock strikes twelve.*)

DOROTHY: So is it goodbye?

SHADOW: Listen—the clock has struck twelve. Up to twelve o'clock tonight I was forbidden by the terms to a bet to disclose who I was, but now I can tell you. My name is Thorton Hart Dudley. I made a bet of five thousand dollars with several New York men whom I met in Philadelphia that I could prove the New York police utterly incompetent, by committing daring robberies, and remain uncaught for two weeks. My two weeks is up now— I am a burglar no longer, and I have won my bet.

DOROTHY: Then you are not a thief?

SHADOW: Miss Connage, I am not in circumstances which put me in want of money. It was simply a question of daring with me. The fancy struck me that I should like to be a burglar for a while, and when I had once entered into an agreement, I stuck it out, and— (*Takes her hand. She draws it away.*)
(*Enter Mr. Connage.*)

MR. C.: Here, here! What's all this?

DOROTHY: Oh Father, this is my friend, Mr.—Mr. Dudley.

MR. C.: (*Surprised.*) Bless me, it's the burglar!

SHADOW: No sir— Never a burglar. Only a Shadow, and a Captured Shadow at that. (*Glances at Dorothy.*)
(*Mr. Connage faints in chair.*)

(*Curtain.*)

END OF PLAY

COSTUMES

Hubert Connage— tuxedo.
The Shadow— dress suit.
Miss Saunders— gray housekeeper's dress, kerchief, and cap and apron.
Mr. Connage— smoking jacket.
Mrs. Connage— dressy house dress and jewels.
Dorothy Connage— evening dress.
Helen Mayburn— evening dress.
Rabbit Simmons— old clothes.
Chinyman Rudd— old clothes, and checked suit later.
Officer McGinness— policeman's suit.
Officer Leon Dureal— policeman's suit.
Emma Kate— black maid's dress, cap, and apron.

Coward

THE Civil War, an early interest of the young Fitzgerald, served as background for this third play as it had for two of his *Now and Then* stories, "The Room With the Green Blinds," an unbelievable tale about John Wilkes Booth, and the earlier "A Debt of Honor," about a young brave Confederate soldier sentenced to death for falling asleep while on sentry duty, receiving a reprieve, and later dying heroically in combat. *Coward*, too, was a study of character, this time about southerner Jim Holworthy who changes from coward to hero and eventually wins the hand of Lindy Douglas—a forerunner of Fitzgerald's later femmes fatales—whose determination is responsible for his going into battle. Jim's cowardly nature and naïveté, some of which is incredible, is set against the actions of Lindy's brother, who steals $12,000 from enemy troops; her father, who though crippled, threatens to fight with a broomstick; and even the children, who are deeply involved in war games. Once again, as in *The Captured Shadow*, Fitzgerald had portrayed a wide range of characters. These include a comically sentimental pair, the romantic Virginia Taylor and the foppish Lieutenant Altwater, the overly proud Angelina Bangs, whose annoyance with the mildly blasphemous, blustering Judge Douglas impels Jim's sarcastic singing of the gospel hymn, "Throw Out the Lifeline," and Jeff, the stereotyped Negro servant. But despite this clutter of characters and subplots, Fitzgerald managed to return to his main theme at the end of the play. And if some of this is too melodramatic—Jim's method of subduing the pillaging soldier, for example, is hard to believe—Fitzgerald's portrayal at the beginning of act two of war's effect on those who stay at home is convincing.

Almost a half century later, Andrew Turnbull interviewed a number of the participants in this play and recorded these recollections in his biography of Fitzgerald. Of the young playwright, Turnbull wrote:

> He knew how to soothe the girl who had only been able to rent one costume for a play whose action extended over several years. (Her mother had suggested her saying, "Here

I am in the same old dress I was wearing when Sumter fell!") Then there was the girl who blushed at the line, "Father, remember your liver!" and the girl who wouldn't say the business about cleaning her nails because it was undignified. All this had to be worked out. When it came to rewriting, Fitzgerald was indefatigable, retiring to a corner and tossing off new lines with his ever-facile pen. As an adlibber he was equally skilled. During the performance at White Bear everyone was waiting for the cue *A shot without*, but no shot came. The boy in charge of firing had discovered at the last minute that his pistol contained a live cartridge instead of a blank. In his alarm he ran down three flights of stairs and out to the end of a pier, where he blasted away into the night. Fitzgerald, on stage at the time, filled the gap quite plausibly by rummaging for a box of cigars. His ingenuity was again tested when one of the actors said, "Here comes Father now," gesturing to the left. Whereupon the old man in his wheelchair hurtled in from the *right*—jet propelled, it would seem, for the stage was a raised platform, and it had taken considerable pushing to get the wheelchair up the ramp.[1]

While some of these events may not have happened exactly this way (the memory of the girl objecting to the discussion of her nails may be from *Assorted Spirits*, for example), they do suggest Fitzgerald's many activities in the production.

[1] Andrew Turnbull, *Scott Fitzgerald* (New York: Scribners, 1962), p. 43.

Coward

By Francis Scott Fitzgerald

Under the direction of Elizabeth Clay Rogers Magoffin

Written for The Elizabethan Dramatic Club

A drama in two acts, given for the benefit of the Baby Welfare Association, and presented at the Saint Paul Y.W.C.A. Auditorium, Friday evening, August 29, 1913.

CAST OF CHARACTERS

JUDGE DOUGLAS	Robert Clark
MRS. DOUGLAS	Alice Lyon
LINDY DOUGLAS	Dorothy Greene
LIEUT. CHARLES DOUGLAS, C.S.A.	Scott Fitzgerald
LIEUT. PERCY ALTWATER, C.S.A.	Gustave Schurmeier
JIM HOLWORTHY	Lawrence Boardman
JEFFERSON	Theodore Parkhouse
CECILIA ASHTON	Eleanor Alair
VIRGINIA TAYLOR	Katherine Schulze
CAPT. ORMSBY, U.S.A.	Wharton Smith
CLARA DOUGLAS	Letitia Magoffin
TOMMY DOUGLAS	Rudolf Patterson
MISS PRUIT	Elizabeth McDavitt
ANGELINA BANGS	Julia Dorr
PRIVATE WILLINGS	Scott Fitzgerald
PRIVATE BARKIS	Gustave Schurmeier
PRIVATE JOHNSON	Robert Clark

(Repeated upon *urgent request* at White Bear Yacht Club, Dellwood, Minnesota, Tuesday evening, September 2, 1913.)

Coward

ACT I

Scene—*Living room in the home of Judge Douglas somewhere in Virginia. Rich furnishings in colonial style of the period.*
Time—*1861.*

(*Discovered at rise of curtain— Judge Douglas, seated in invalid chair. Mrs. Douglas near him. Judge Douglas seems to be disturbed about something. In his hand he shakes a bouquet of fresh flowers.*)

JUDGE D.: I tell you I won't have it! I can't have it!

MRS. D.: I'm sure he's a good boy.

JUDGE D.: Good? Good be hanged! I'd rather see him a human devil and off to the war, than hanging around here when every able-bodied man in the South is fighting. If I were able to walk I'd be there against the Yanks if I had only a broomstick. And the idea of that impudent young jackanapes paying attention to our daughter Lindy!— Bah!

MRS. D.: Well, I'm sure she doesn't encourage him.

JUDGE D.: That's not to her credit. If she did encourage him she'd be a lunatic.

MRS. D.: Arthur!

JUDGE D.: That's what she'd be—a lunatic.

MRS. D.: But she hasn't encouraged him.

JUDGE D.: Then why did he send her these? Why, tell me?

MRS. D.: I'm sure I don't know.

JUDGE D.: Call in Jeff. I'll show him!

MRS. D.: (*Rings bell.*)
(*Enter Jeff.*)

JUDGE D.: Throw these in the ash barrel, and any more from young Jim Holworthy as well. I'll have no stay-at-homes making love to my daughter.

MRS. D.: I'm sure Lindy will see that a young man like that is not for her to become intimate with, but I see no harm in her seeing him.

JUDGE D.: But I do. Ned Holworthy himself said to me that he considered his son Jim a disgrace to his family. Why didn't he enlist with my Charley and the rest?

JEFF: Dere's somebody comin'. (*Looking out window.*)

MRS. D.: I suppose it's the mail.

JEFF: No'm, it's a female—two of 'em. (*Starts to leave.*)

JUDGE D.: Where's that Jeff? Where is he? Ring the bell. Oh, there you are. I can't talk to Lindy now. I'm liable to use violent language.

MRS. D.: Wheel Mr. Douglas to the side veranda and then leave him. He is testy today.

(*Exit Jeff wheeling Judge Douglas in chair.*)

(*Enter Lindy, followed by Cecilia.*)

LINDY: (*In doorway.*) Goodbye Ellen. Goodbye Miss Hazelton.

MRS. D.: That you, Lindy?

LINDY: Yes Mother.

MRS. D.: Oh, hello Cecilia.

CECILIA: Good morning, Mrs. Douglas. How's everybody over here?

MRS. D.: All well. How's your Mother, Cecilia?

CECILIA: She hasn't been the same since John was shot.

MRS. D.: (*Sighs.*) Ah yes, I know. Charley's well—praise be to heaven—but one son is not too much to give to the cause. Tommy would go if he were only old enough.

LINDY: Let's not be doleful, Mother. I reckon I've got troubles enough. Look— (*Holding out sewing.*) Uniforms to make for Charley. How he can ever wear through a cloth this thick is a mystery to me, and yet they do—and always want more.

MRS. D.: Lindy, that's no way to talk— You may be thankful you still have a brother to sew for.

LINDY: Well, I can't help it— It is annoying! It's sew, sew, sew— I wish I were a man or at least as small as Tommy so that I could pretend I was.

CECILIA: Mrs. Douglas, what do you think? This morning I got all dressed for riding, boots and all, came down stairs and found that Kate, my new saddle horse, was gone.

MRS. D. and LINDY: Stolen?

CECILIA: No, sent ahead to the Army. I guess I'll be a pedestrian till Jeff Davis sits in Washington.

LINDY: Which will be a long while, I am afraid.

(*Outside a fife is heard. Enter Tommy and Clara Douglas dressed as soldiers, Miss Pruit, their governess, following, carrying gun.*)

TOMMY: Halt! Good morning, lady. You haven't a pair of shoes for a poor old campaigner, have you? I haven't eaten anything but salt pork since Bull Run.

CLARA: You ain't going to eat shoes, are you?

TOMMY: Silence, Private Clara! If you speak again, I'll make you the camp followers and advance Miss Pruit to the main army.

MISS PRUIT: Mrs. Douglas, do I have to stand for this? I've been the camp followers and the deserters and the Northerners all day. I wish I had remained in Boston as my folks advised, but I wouldn't take the trip now for the Pilgrim Fathers themselves.

CECILIA: There aren't going to be Pilgrim Fathers much longer, Miss Pruit.

MISS PRUIT: I want you to know, Miss Ashton, that my cousin's aunt's grandmother on my father's side is related to Governor Bradford of New York.

CECILIA and LINDY: Oh excuse us, Miss Pruit!

TOMMY: Major Douglas, I think she's a spy. If I mistake not, Boston is somewhere in Pennsylvania?

CLARA: You're right.

TOMMY: To the guard house. Charge! (*They charge on Miss Pruit, and all exit.*)

LINDY: I guess they've all got the war spirit.

(*Enter Angelina Bangs.*)

ANGELINA: Good morning.

MRS. D.: Angelina. Come in.

ANGELINA: If I may. I am perusing a most attractive little book.

CECILIA: So?

ANGELINA: Yes.

LINDY: What is it?

ANGELINA: The life of St. Cecilia. Your namesake, dear friend.

CECILIA: Here comes a sermon.

ANGELINA: Such a sweet book!

LINDY: And so dry! !

MRS. D.: Lindy, I've often wished that you were more like Angelina.

ANGELINA: I wish every one was.

CECILIA: Generous creature!

MRS. D.: Cecilia!!

ANGELINA: I have already forgiven her. You should learn, dear girl, not to be hasty.

MRS. D.: There's something for you to practice, Lindy.

LINDY: But I can't be sanctimonious.

ANGELINA: But you can try. I, alas, have had hard struggles. I inherit all the low impulses of my father's family, the Bangs. It is a continual struggle for the Angeline to overcome the Bangs. Alas, the Bangs often overcomes. This morning—I confess it with a tear of shame—I came very close to exclaiming "Rats!" in an ill-natured manner.

CECILIA: Oh do tell us. Did the Bangs win?

ANGELINA: No, the Angelina conquered.

LINDY: I'm so glad.

ANGELINA: I must be going, Mrs. Douglas. Goodbye. Children, you have my prayers.

(*Exit.*)

LINDY: What a sanctimonious creature!

CECILIA: I'd like to see the Bangs get out just once.

LINDY: It never will.

CECILIA: Oh Mrs. Douglas, will you show me that pattern for the coats?

MRS. D.: Certainly Celia; I've been meaning to. Come upstairs. (*Turns toward door leading to hall.*)

(*Enter Jeff. He sees that Lindy is not alone, so retreats in haste.*)

MRS. D.: I wonder what he wanted?

LINDY: Probably wants to sample some of Daddy's cigars.

(*Exit Mrs. Douglas and Cecilia.*)

(*Enter Jeff, cautiously.*)

JEFF: Ex-excuse me, Miss Lindy, bu-but dere's a personal mattah I got to broach to you.

LINDY: All right Jeff, what is it?

JEFF: Dere's a gemmen outside said he'd relieve ma present pecuniary emba'ssment if ah'd give yoh dis here note. He ain't no friend o' yoh father's.

LINDY: Oh, it's Mr. Jim Holworthy. (*Reads note.*) He wants to see me. Show him in.

JEFF: Yassum.

(*Exit Jeff.*)

(*Enter Jeff, followed by Jim Holworthy.*)

JEFF: I renounce Mistah James Holworthy.
JIM: Ah—ah— — Morning, Miss Lindy.
LINDY: Good morning, Mr. Holworthy.
JIM: I—ah—just happened to be passing, so I thought I'd say "hello" with you.
LINDY: Hello.
JIM: Hello. I guess I'll be going.
LINDY: Won't you sit down? Take Mr. Holworthy's hat, Jeff.
(*Jeff starts to take hat.*)
JIM: Hey there, what are you doing?
LINDY: It's all right, Mr. Holworthy.
JIM: Sit down. Well, up—that is, begging your pardon. (*Gets up and reaches for hat.*)
LINDY: You may go, Jeff.
JEFF: Yassum.
LINDY: Jeff!
JEFF: Yassum, I'm agoin'. Mistah Holworthy ain't forgot sumpin, is he?
JIM: Oh yes. Hmm—ah— (*Fumbles in pockets.*) Can you change ten cents, Miss Lindy?
LINDY: (*Shakes her head.*)
JIM: Well, here's the money. It's more than I intended. (*Gives money to Jeff.*)
JEFF: Ten cents Confederate!
LINDY: Jeff, go out at once!
(*Exit Jeff.*)
JIM: If there ain't ten cents gone quick!
LINDY: That's too bad, Mr. Holworthy.
JIM: Yes, it is.
(*Pause.*)
Are you feeling well?
LINDY: Pretty well, thank you. How are you?
JIM: I reckon I'm all right; how are you?— — I mean—oh you're all right—you just said so.
LINDY: Yes.
(*Pause.*)
JIM: How's your mother?
LINDY: Fine.
JIM: Your father?
LINDY: Fine, thank you.

JIM: Your little sister?
LINDY: She's all right.
JIM: And your brother?
LINDY: He's right well.
JIM: Ain't there a governess?
LINDY: Yes.
JIM: How's she?
LINDY: Fine.
(*Pause.*)
JIM: How are all the niggers?
LINDY: All right, I reckon.
JIM: That's good. You're all right, ain't you?
LINDY: Oh yes, thank you.
(*Pause.*)
JIM: Ah—ha! ha! (*Laughs.*)
LINDY: Are you ill?
JIM: Ill— Me? No, I ain't sick.
LINDY: Then what are you laughing at?
JIM: Did you get those flowers I sent you?
LINDY: Flowers?
JIM: Yes, flowers.
LINDY: What flowers?
JIM: The ones I sent you.
LINDY: Why no. (*Rings.*) That's powerful funny!
JIM: Didn't you get them? I left them at the door.
(*Enter Jeff.*)
LINDY: Jeff, did I get some flowers this morning?
JEFF: Well, not exactly— You didn't get 'em, you received 'em.
LINDY: Where are they?
JEFF: Why, yoh fathah—yoh fathah, he—he done planted 'em.
LINDY: Where? Where?
JEFF: (*Waves both hands.*) Oh, all 'round.
LINDY: Where, Jeff?
JEFF: In de—in de ash can.
JIM: They ain't going to grow in the ash can, Miss Lindy. No kind of flowers going to grow in the ash can.
LINDY: You may go, Jeff.
JIM: I reckon those flowers are ruined. I suspicion your father ain't over crazy about me somehow.
LINDY: So?

JIM: Yes. No man that grows flowers is going to plant them in an ash can unless he doesn't want them to grow, Miss Lindy.

LINDY: How astute you are.

JIM: As-tute?

LINDY: Clever.

JIM: Oh yes, I am rather clever, but I don't know—they don't seem to care overmuch for me around here somehow.

LINDY: They don't?

JIM: Father wanted me to go to war, but I didn't care about it particularly. By the way, Miss Lindy, I've got a little matter I'd like to speak to you about.

LINDY: What's that?

JIM: Do you want to get married?

LINDY: Eventually, I reckon. Why?

JIM: Oh, I just wondered.

LINDY: (*Smiles.*)

JIM: What do you think of me?

LINDY: What do I think of you?

JIM: Yes, for a husband.

LINDY: I reckon you'd make a good husband.

JIM: You do?— Say, that's fine. Well Lindy—

LINDY: *Miss* Lindy!

JIM: Why, ain't we engaged?

LINDY: (*Laughing.*) Oh horrors, no! I didn't say a good husband for me. I said a good husband for somebody else.

JIM: (*Crestfallen.*) Then—then say you'll be a sister to me.

LINDY: Why?

JIM: I was reading a story the other day, and the lady said she'd be a sister to the man she turned down.

LINDY: I'm afraid I can't.

JIM: Well, could you be an aunt or a grandmother?

LINDY: Mr. Holworthy, my advice to you is right here:— Before you come around proposing to a girl, you had better go out with my brother and the rest and do some fighting. Then people would have some use for you. Do you know why my father doesn't like you?

JIM: Mmm—

LINDY: He thinks you are a coward.

JIM: (*Calmly.*) Does he?

LINDY: You're a fine one! You sit right there and let me call you a coward, with no remonstrance?

JIM: What do you want me to do?— Hit you?

LINDY: Why didn't you enlist when the rest did?

JIM: I thought one man wouldn't make any difference and I didn't care particularly how the war came out anyway, and there were plenty to go without me.

LINDY: Every man counts, Mr. Holworthy, and I and everyone else would respect you more if you had joined the army.

JIM: Do you really think so, Miss Lindy?

LINDY: Yes I do.

JIM: (*Starting to go.*) Well, goodbye.

LINDY: Where are you going?

JIM: I'm going to enlist.

(*Exit Jim.*)

(*Enter Virginia on run.*)

VIRGINIA: Oh Lindy, news, news! Our army is retreating and will pass by here within half an hour by the Royd Turnpike.

LINDY: And Charley's regiment?

VIRGINIA: Your brother's regiment is with them.

LINDY: Oh, what news! Mother! Mother! (*Calling.*)

MRS. D.: (*Outside.*) Yes Lindy?

LINDY: Come down quick. Virginia, how do you know?

VIRGINIA: The advance guard is already in sight. My little brother Dick rode out to make sure, and he was right. It's Early's division of Lee's army.

(*Enter Mrs. Douglas and Cecilia.*)

MRS. D.: What's the matter, Lindy? Oh, howdy, Virginia.

VIRGINIA: The army! Oh the army! Celia, rejoice, rejoice! Charley is coming home. Isn't it perfectly romantic!

MRS. D.: For an hour perhaps.

VIRGINIA: (*Sits at piano and plays "Away Down South in Dixie."*)

(*Enter Tommy and Clara Douglas and Governess.*)

TOMMY: Oh Mother, may I go out and see the soldiers? May I? May I? (*Jumping with excitement.*)

CLARA: Yes Mother, may I?

MRS. D.: Very well, children.

CLARA:
TOMMY: } Thanks, Mother.

(*Exit Tommy and Clara on run.*)

(*Hoofbeats heard outside.*)

(*Enter Charley, followed by Percy.*)

CHARLEY: Well Mother, I'm back again, Sister too, and Celia. (*Embraces them all in turn.*) Mother, this is my friend, Lieutenant Altwater. He's an English sympathizer who came over and joined us.

MRS. D.:
CECILIA:
VIRGINIA:
LINDY: } We're glad to meet you, Lieutenant Altwater. (*Etc.*)

PERCY: Delighted, I'm sure. You know, I haven't seen a girl for six months. I declare I thought I'd die! You know, I love the girls, and alas they return the compliment.

VIRGINIA: (*Thrilled.*) Oh, are you a sharpshooter?

PERCY: Me? No, no, I'm in the Infantry, mounted at present.

CECILIA: Infant? Infant? A regiment of very young men?

PERCY: No, no, — Those on foot— Anyone on foot.

CECILIA: Oh girls, then we're all infantries. (*Laughs.*)

VIRGINIA: How perfectly romantic!

MRS. D.: How do you like the army, Mr. Altwater.

PERCY: Very well, except for the servants. You know, they object to my keeping two valets. Isn't it outrageous? I started out with a manicure lady but she eloped with my footman. Then my groom drank some of that bully Kentucky whiskey, and alas I don't know where he is now!

VIRGINIA: How deliciously sentimental! Come, would you not like to see the place?

PERCY: I'd love to. (*Extends arm to Virginia.*) It reminds me of an old shooting lodge I've got up in Suffolk.
(*Exit Percy and Virginia.*)

CHARLEY: Well Mother, we're rich. Our cavalry company fell in with a Yankee commissary train and here are twelve thousand dollars Union money. That's shoes, guns, and what not for our whole division. Looks good to us. I'm acting commissary since old Wilkins was shot. Twelve thousand! That helps along.

LINDY: How long can you stay, Charley?

CHARLEY: Five minutes more. The division has passed now, and the Union advance is right behind us. But where is Father?
(*Enter Judge Douglas, wheeled by Jeff.*)

JUDGE D.: My son!

CHARLEY: Father! (*They clasp hands.*)

JUDGE D.: Well, I'm mighty glad to see you. You don't look any the worse for wear.

CHARLEY: I've been fine— A little scratch on my forehead— Nothing to speak of.

GIRLS and MRS. D.: Oh!

CHARLEY: Hardly drew blood, I assure you.

JUDGE D.: Charley, you are just in time to tell your sister what kind of a man Jim Holworthy is. He's been sending her flowers.

CHARLEY: Jim Holworthy been sending Lindy flowers? Why Lindy, do you know that that man is a rank quitter? He's a stay-at-home! The day we organized our company he refused to join, and wouldn't give any reason. He's—he's—why—if he does it again I'll take him out and horsewhip him!

LINDY: There, there, Charley, your little sister is quite old enough to take care of herself. Mr. Holworthy has just enlisted at my bidding.

CHARLEY: I didn't know he had the nerve.

JUDGE D.: Oh, so you've seen him lately, have you? I'll cane him!

LINDY: There, Father, it's all right.

JUDGE D.: But I tell you it isn't all right! He can't— —

(*Enter Percy.*)

(*Exit Judge Douglas and Jeff.*)

PERCY: Charley old sport, we'd better be going. We're behind the column now, and the Yankee outriders are not far behind.

CHARLEY: I reckon you're right, Percy.

PERCY: You'll excuse us, Mrs. Douglas. You know, General Lee really needs me. I fancy he's wondering now where I am. I'm rather the power behind the throne, you know.

CHARLEY: Well, goodbye Celia; goodbye Lindy; goodbye Mother.

PERCY: Good afternoon Mrs. Douglas. Sorry I haven't a card with me.

(*Enter Judge Douglas and Jeff.*)

JEFF: Mistah Charley, dere's a squad of Yanks jumpin' over the fence down by de cow pasture and comin' up here right pert!

CHARLEY: All right, Jeff. You haven't a few cigars, Father? We don't get such luxuries.

JUDGE D.: Here— Help yourself.

CHARLEY: (*Takes cigars.*) Here, Percy.

PERCY: If I may. (*Also takes cigars.*)

MRS. D.: Do hurry, Charley; I'm so afraid.

CHARLEY: Goodbye everyone. Come on Percy.

(*Exit Charley and Percy.*)

(*Sound of hoofbeats. Voice outside.*)

Hey, halt there! (*Two shots fired.*)

MRS. D.: Oh!

CECILIA: (*At window.*) They're safe. Charley is waving his hat.

MRS. D.: Oh, thank God for that!

CECILIA: Some Yanks are coming across the yard.

JUDGE D.: Oh, if I wasn't a cripple! Oh!!

(*Door opens—*)

(*Enter Captain Ormsby with Privates.*)

CAPT. O.: Good morning.

(*No answer.*)

You don't seem sociable. Well, don't answer then, but listen. A few officers will have to be quartered on you tonight. I'm sorry, lady— I thought I'd prepare you. It's a disagreeable duty.

LINDY: We need no sympathy from Yanks.

MRS. D.: None at all.

CECILIA: I think I'll be going home, Mrs. Douglas.

MRS. D.: }
LINDY: } Goodbye, Celia.

CECILIA: Goodbye.

(*Exit Cecilia.*)

CAPT. O.: (*Looking at Judge Douglas in chair.*) What's this? A Southerner and not at war?

JUDGE D.: Your remarks, sir, are entirely out of place. I'll have you know, sir, that I—I—

LINDY: My father is paralyzed from his waist down.

CAPT. O.: I see. Well, you may expect the officers for dinner.

MRS. D.: If we must, we must. How many?

CAPT. O.: Four.

MRS. D.: The pantry is open— They can serve themselves. I will wait on no Yankees.

CAPT. O.: By the way, who were those two Rebs that rode away just as we came up?

JUDGE D.: That is our affair.

CAPT. O.: There're a pesky lot of cavalrymen. They robbed a commissary train this morning, and cost Uncle Sam twelve thousand in greenbacks.

JUDGE D.: That doesn't concern me in the slightest. Jeff, wheel me out. Come on, Mary.

(*Exit Judge Douglas, Mrs. Douglas, and Jeff.*)

CAPT. O.: I'll put a guard in front of the house, Miss Douglas, to keep the soldiers from annexing food.

LINDY: As you please.

(*Exit Captain Ormsby.*)

LINDY: (*Goes to table and picks up work. Under it she finds the money. She hides it under cover.*)

JIM: (*Outside.*) I don't know any countersign— I ain't ever been behind a counter anyhow. I ain't no clerk.

PRIVATE WILLINGS: (*Outside.*) I tell you you can't pass.

(*Enter Jim Holworthy, followed by Private Willings.*)

LINDY: Well, Mr. Holworthy, did you did it? Did you en—

JIM: Hobble gobble gobble!

LINDY: Why, what's the matter? I only wanted to know if you en—

JIM: Hobble gobble!

PRIVATE W.: What's the matter? Is this some plot?

JIM: No. You see, she's got a cold, and she wanted me to go to the drugstore and get her a mustard plaster.

LINDY: Why—

JIM: For her dog. You see, she's fond of the dog, and it caught the cold.

LINDY: Mr. Holworthy, it's no such thing— I just wanted to know if you—if you—

JIM: Aber-ca-daber!

PRIVATE W.: This is treason. I heard him say, "I could have had you." You're a spy.

JIM: No, I ain't.

LINDY: This man isn't a spy— He's just afraid to go to war.

PRIVATE W.: Well, I'll believe you, mum. But don't let me see you snooping around here, Rube!

(*Exit Private Willings.*)

JIM: Did you hear what he called me? Come back here, you— I'll show him. I'll—I'll— (*Makes motion of stabbing.*)

(*Enter Private Willings.*)

PRIVATE W.: Did you call?

JIM: Me? No, I didn't call. Me? Oh, oh, I didn't call.

PRIVATE W.: Excuse me, lady.

(*Exit Private Willings.*)

LINDY: Well, did you enlist?

JIM: Almost. I tossed a coin to see which army I'd join.

LINDY: Horrors! Who won?

JIM: Don't be afraid, the South won me.

LINDY: And did you enlist?

JIM: Well, the recruiting officer had fled south with the Southern army, so I thought I'd try the Yanks, but they had a picture in a book on the table—

LINDY: A picture?

JIM: All blood. It was a battle. And—and then I realized that I'd better wait and join the other side, so I told the man to wait for me.

LINDY: Mr. Jim Holworthy, never speak to me again! I told my family I had influenced you to enlist, and—and—they believed me, and now you didn't! I think you are contemptible— —

JIM: Excuse me.

(*Enter Judge Douglas wheeled by Jeff.*)

JUDGE D.: What's this? What's this? Tell me, what's this? On my honor it's the worm!

JIM: Worm?

JUDGE D.: You impertinent young scamp, calling on my daughter. I'll—I'll cane you! Jeff—my cane! Wheel me at him! (*Jeff starts to wheel and Jim retreats.*)

JIM: Oh Judge Douglas, be reasonable.

LINDY: Father, you'll have a fit! Remember your liver is in poor condition.

JIM: Look out, Judge, there ain't anything like a good liver.

JUDGE D.: What do you know about my liver? Lindy did you ever mention my liver to him?

LINDY: Never, Father— (*Cautioning.*) But your liver—

JUDGE D.: Bother my liver.

JIM: Well, don't bother me.

(*Enter Angelina.*)

ANGELINA: A family disagreement? How perfectly shocking. Our family never squabble.

JUDGE D.: What's this? Do you, young lady, mean to dictate to me in my own house?—

LINDY: Go slow, Father.

ANGELINA: Oh the Bangs in me is rising. Oh can I stop it? Can I? (*Struggle.*) There. I have conquered it. Angeline stands victorious.

F. Scott Fitzgerald, c. 1915.

Elizabeth Magoffin's transcription of *The Girl from Lazy J*, with drawing of cast, possibly by Dorothy Greene.

Elizabeth Magoffin.

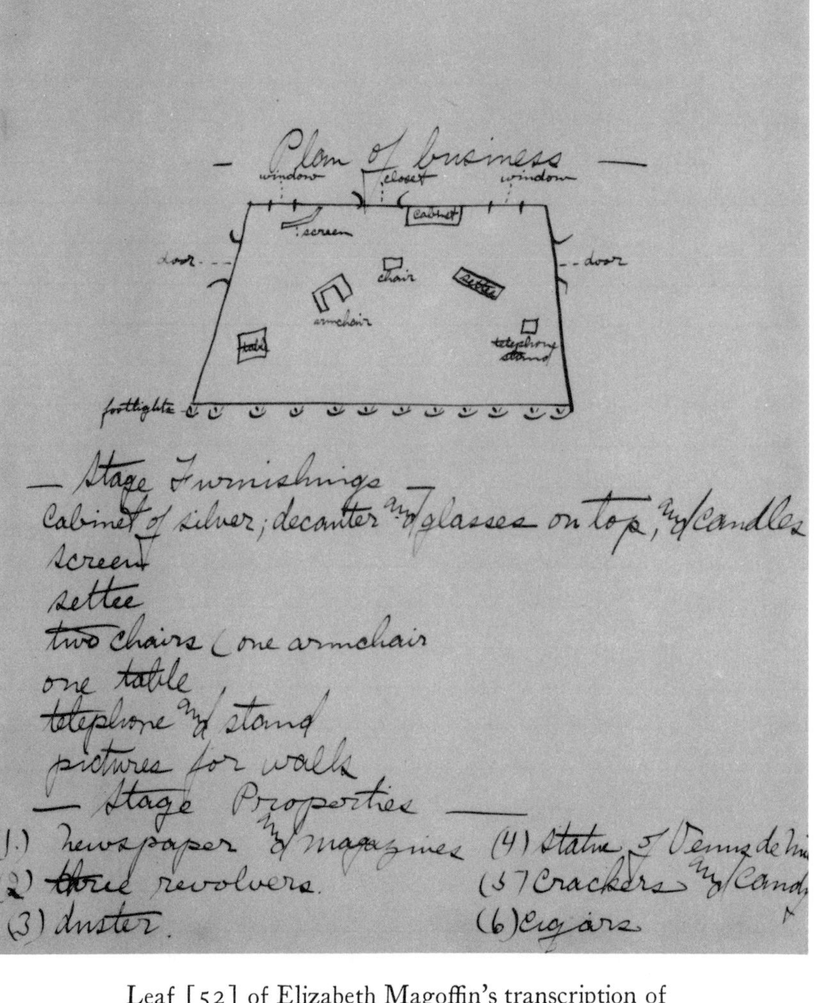
— Plan of business —

window
closet
window
cabinet
screen
door
door
chair
settee
armchair
table
telephone stand
footlights

— Stage Furnishings —

Cabinet of silver; decanter w/ glasses on top; w/ candles
screen
settee
~~two~~ chairs (one armchair
one table
~~telephone~~ w/ stand
pictures for walls

— Stage Properties —

(1.) newspaper w/ magazines
(2) ~~three~~ revolvers.
(3) duster.
(4) Statue of Venus de Mi[lo]
(5) Crackers w/ Candy
(6) Cigars

Leaf [52] of Elizabeth Magoffin's transcription of *The Captured Shadow.*

Stage Furnishings

Small table – Side table – settee – piano – piano bench – linen chest – two chairs – invalid wheel chair.

exit
exit
exit
chest
side table
chair
settee
inv. chair
chair
table
piano

Stage Properties

Jug of milk
Jug of water
Two glasses
Two crackers
Bonnet of flowers
Tablecloth
Bell for table

Roll of money
Letter for "Dell"
Sewing for "Lindy"
Necklace for "Lindy"
Book for "Angelina"
Cane for "Judge Douglas"
Vase
Two plates

Umbrella } for "Clara"
Broom } for "Tommy"
Monocle for "Percy"
Two Oranges
Two Pistols & Cartridge Belt
Two Rifles
Two paper hats

Costumes

Judge Douglas — Frock coat, brocaded vest, stock, light trousers, wig, beard, mustac[he]

Mrs. Douglas – / Cecelia Ashton / Virginia Taylor / Lindy Douglas / Angelina Bangs } Typical war-time (1861) gowns for house. (A variety of colors & styles preferable) Curls in hair

Lieut. Charles Douglas / Lieut. Percy Astwater } Confederate uniforms.

Capt. James Holworthy – Farm clothes in first act, confederate uniform in second a[ct]

Capt. Ormsby / Private Willings / " Barkis / " Johnson } Union uniforms.

Jefferson – Darkey make-up, butlers coat, red vest, black trousers, white sox.

Miss Primt – Gray or black governess uniform. "Old maid" coiffure & spectacle[s]

Clara Douglas / Tommy Douglas } Typical children's suits of period.

Recto of final unpaginated leaf of Elizabeth Magoffin's transcription of *Coward*.

Gustave B. Schurmeier
PRESENTS
LAURANCE BOARDMAN
IN
Scott Fitzgerald's Comedy
"THE COWARD"
AT THE
Y. W. C. A.--August 29, 1913

Tickets 25c ‖ ON SALE AT Y. W. C. A. and Y. M. C. A.

Given for the Benefit of the Baby Welfare

Poster for *Coward*. Original is black on yellow.

Fitzgerald as Lieutenant Charles Douglas (third from right) at rehearsal of *Coward*.

"Assorted Spirits"

A Comedy in Two Acts by Scott Fitzgerald
Presented by the
ELIZABETHAN DRAMATIC CLUB
For the Benefit of the
BABY WELFARE ASSOCIATION

Cast

William Chapman	Gustave Schurmeier
Peter Wetherby	Scott Fitzgerald
Dickie Wetherby	James Armstrong
Josephus Hendrix	John Mitchell
Muligan, Policeman	Robert Clark
O'Flanagan, Policeman	MacNeil Seymore
Cecile Wetherby	Elenore Alair
Clara King	Katherine Schulze
Madame Zada	Alice Lyon
Miss Spigot	Margaret Armstrong
Second-Story Sal	Dorothy Greene
Hulda	Betty Mudge

ACT I—The Wetherby House. 9:30 P. M.
ACT II—Same. Next Morning.

CURTAIN RAISER

Maxixe - - - By Mr. Mayall Brunner and Miss Katherine Schulze

STAFF

Directress—Miss Elizabeth Magoffin.
Stage Manager—Mr. Scott F. Fitzgerald.
Gen. Business Manager—Mr. G. B. Schurmeier.
Treasurer—Mr. John L. Mitchell.

Costumes by Giesen — Music by Pier

Program for *Assorted Spirits.*

JUDGE D.: What's this? Bangs, Angelina? Why the Bangs in you is the best part of you. Why Georgie Bangs ever married that patron saint mother of yours beats me. And you (*turning to Jim*), you're a pair— I can't control myself— I'll burst! Wheel me out Jeff— No, don't! Go ahead! Young sir— Stop! If I ever— Keep going!—see you again— Stop I say! I'll— I'll thrash you—

(*Exit Judge Douglas, growling, wheeled by Jeff.*)

ANGELINA: His words are blasphemous. I am shocked. I will return home and pray that he will never regret this moment. (*Exit.*)

JIM: (*Sings.*) "Throw out the life line."

He ain't pleasant somehow. You know, he doesn't love me.

LINDY: No he doesn't. (*Whistle heard outside.*) That's my brother's whistle that we used when we were children. He's—he's in the house! He's coming back! Heavens!! And the Yankees everywhere. Oh Charley, Charley. (*Whistles.*) Where's the sentry?

JIM: On the other end of the veranda.

(*Enter Charley.*)

LINDY: Charley, what brings you here? The Yankees are all around the house. There is a guard on the doorstep. Oh go, before it is too late.

CHARLEY: I came back for—

JIM: (*Stepping up.*) Howdy do, Charley.

(*Charley snubs him.*)

CHARLEY: So this is your resource when your friends are in the army?—this—this stay-at-home!

LINDY: We won't quarrel now.

CHARLEY: I'm sorry, Lindy. But I must hurry. I mislaid that money. Where is it?

LINDY: Here it is. (*Gets money from under cover.*)

Take it and go!

(*Voice outside.*)

CAPT. O.: Has no one gone in or out?

LINDY: (*To Charley, motioning him to door.*) Quick! Go out here.

(*Exit Charley.*)

(*Enter Captain Ormsby.*)

CAPT. O.: Good morning, Miss Douglas; my duty is most unpleasant. There is a man concealed here. My sergeant saw a horseman ride through the gap and leave his horse in the woods. He was seen entering here.

LINDY: I'm afraid you are mistaken.

Capt. O.: I sincerely hope so. Still, I am forced to assure myself of it.

Lindy: There is no one here.

Capt. O.: You will kindly stand aside. It is hardly my pleasure to disobey a lady.

(*Enter Charles Douglas, revolver in hand.*)

Charley: I will save you that trouble. Hands up, Captain.

Capt. O.: (*Raises hands.*) I have men at this very doorstep. I have but to raise my voice.

Charley: And you'll be raising it with the angel chorus, or as you are a Yankee, contrarywise, if you say another word.

Lindy: Charley, what shall I do? (*Pulling him to side.*)

Charley: (*Aside to Lindy.*) I'll have to hide here. Get him out of here first. (*To Yankee.*) Yank, right about face. You walk from here right down to the gate without looking behind. A sign to your men and you go— (*Still pointing pistol at him.*)

Capt. O.: Your chances are one in a million.

Charley: No remarks. March!

(*Exit Captain Ormsby.*)

Lindy: Quick—open this. (*Pointing to chest.*) Charley, quick—get in. Now slam that door. (*to Jim*)

(*Voices heard outside, and tramping.*)

Capt. O.: Here they are.

(*Enter Capt. Ormsby, Private Willings, and Private Barkis.*)

Quick— Through the house! He can't get away.

(*Exit Privates.*)

(*Turning to Jim.*) So you're a pal of his, are you? In plain clothes— You'll swing for this. He's in uniform—lucky beggar.

Jim: No, I ain't.

Capt. O.: And you, young lady, may have to eat prison fare for a while. This is high treason.

Lindy: You dare—you—

Jim: Let him alone, Miss Lindy. He'll get mad.

(*Enter Private Willings.*)

Private W.: No trace of him, sir. Three men are still searching. He must be here.

Capt. O.: I'll get that fresh Reb. Where is he?— Tell me!

Lindy: Do you think you can frighten me?

Capt. O.: Here is a man we can. (*Going towards Jim.*) If you are wise you will say.

JIM: I—I—he—
LINDY: Jim!
CAPT. O.: Where is he?
JIM: I don't know.
CAPT. O.: (*To soldier.*) Give this fellow a lash or two and then— Well, there are ropes in camp.
(*Soldier grabs Jim.*)
JIM: Don't! I—I—
CAPT. O.: Hurry.
LINDY: Jim!
JIM: I—oh, I can't!
CAPT. O.: Away with him.
JIM: Stop! I'll tell. He's—he's in there. (*Pointing to chest. Soldier springs to it and takes out Charley.*)
CHARLEY: You damn coward!
CAPT. O.: (*To Jim.*) Here— Here's a quarter. Southern manhood!
LINDY: (*Crying.*) Goodbye Charley. Oh, my brother.
CHARLEY: I'm only a prisoner of war, Lindy.
CAPT. O.: Right about face— March!
(*Exit Captain Ormsby, Charles Douglas and Private Willings.*)
JIM: Gee, they're taking him away! They almost took me. Well, that's over. What's the matter? Why—why—you ain't mad, are you, Miss Lindy? I—I—oh, I see, I shouldn't have told, but I didn't know. I didn't—as God sees me, I didn't! I was afraid. Speak to me, Miss Lindy. I just had to tell! Oh, don't think I'm a—traitor. Don't, Miss Lindy— Don't!—oh don't! (*Stiffens up.*) I reckon I see now. I'm a—a what he called me, a coward! (*Pause.*) Goodbye, I'm going now, south to the army. I see now, I'm—I'm— — Goodbye, Miss Lindy— Goodbye.
(*Lindy turns and leaves him without an answer.*)

(*Curtain.*)

ACT II

(*Scene same as Act I, and three years later.*)
(*Curtain rises showing Jeff setting table. He gets milk in a jug and fills two glasses half full. Then he gets water jug and fills up the rest of the glasses. Surveys his table. Places four crackers at plates. Then puts flowers in center. Something is lacking so he*

removes four flowers and places them at each plate. Surveys table again with satisfaction.)

(*Enter Mrs. Douglas.*)

MRS. D.: Good morning, Jeff.

JEFF: Mawnin', Mrs. Douglas. (*Hints at table with evident pride.*)

MRS. D.: What's this?

JEFF: De—de luncheon, Mrs. Douglas.

MRS. D.: You surely don't expect us to eat flowers.

JEFF: No'm— No'm— You kin if you wants to, but I don't advise you to. Dey's not good to eat, 'ceptin' maybe cauliflower or bakin' flour.

MRS. D.: And is there nothing else in the ice house?

JEFF: Oh, yassum— Yessam— Dey's lots! Dey's—ah—three or four pieces of bread and one of 'em still pretty good. An—an—half a jug o' milk, an—an—a egg an—a apple— — All that!

MRS. D.: I reckon we're mighty poor, Jeff.

JEFF: Don't talk that way, Mrs. Douglas! Dat ain't no way to talk. Times'll mend—but dis here coat won't.

MRS. D.: Yes, it is well to be hopeful, but I trust the horrible war is almost over. Since the Judge died we've been pretty poor, and Charley, though he has escaped so far, is still there.

JEFF: But you got a daughter.

MRS. D.: Poor Lindy! Having to give up all and become a school teacher. She practically supports us now, Jeff.

JEFF: Ah expect dey'll be a heap o' offers for her when de young men gits home from de wah.

MRS. D.: Jeff— You mustn't talk that way.

JEFF: Yassum— Excuse me. (*Goes to window.*) Dere's Miss Lindy now.

(*Exit Jeff.*)

(*Enter Lindy and Cecilia.*)

LINDY: Hello, Mother. (*Removes shawl and hat.*)

CECILIA: Good morning, Mrs. Douglas.

MRS. D.: Good morning, Celia.

CECILIA: I met Lindy on the way back from her schoolhouse, surrounded by a most adoring crowd of little nuisances. I rescued her, and here we are.

MRS. D.: Did you have a good day, Lindy?

LINDY: Fine, Mother. I think it will be all right now that that Tompkins boy has decided to behave. Mrs. Tompkins sent a note with him this morning authorizing me to punish him to the fullest extent of the law, and when I punish!— I tell you, Mother, I'm growing strong.

MRS. D.: Oh, if Charley were only here to take the burden of supporting us off your shoulders.

CECILIA: I reckon he will soon. Our army is getting weaker and weaker. They're going to make a stand at Appomattox, so Eddie Randolph wrote his mother.

LINDY: We haven't seen Charley for two years.

MRS. D.: I miss him, oh, how I miss him!

LINDY: We can only wait for him. I'll be back, Celia.

(*Exit Lindy.*)

CECILIA: You are not the only one who misses him.

MRS. D.: Celia, I thought so! So you are engaged?

CECILIA: He has asked me to marry him. He wrote me and said that his first duty was to you. He spoke also of Captain Holworthy. He was awarded a medal at the battle of Petersburg.

MRS. D.: Holworthy? Jim Holworthy?

CECILIA: Yes, I reckon he's changed some. He wasn't very popular when he left here, but somehow he joined the army, and he has proved himself.

MRS. D.: But does Charley like him after what happened that time three years ago in this very house, when he was captured through this Holworthy's cowardice?

CECILIA: Charley bears no resentment. Holworthy has saved his life since then. I'm sure I'm willing to accept him as all right if he comes home.

MRS. D.: Perhaps you're right.

CECILIA: And Mrs. Douglas, Charley wrote something else about him—a curious thing— The day Holworthy saved his life—it was in a skirmish—he was wounded slightly, and Charley, in unbuttoning his collar to give him air, saw a locket spring open that he was wearing around his neck. Before he closed it he noticed the picture inside. Holworthy saw that Charley knew, and blushed, saying it was a hobby of his. But Charley knew that Captain Holworthy was carrying Lindy's picture. I've often wondered if she has forgiven him.

LINDY: (*From the doorway.*) Yes, she has forgiven him.

(*Enter Lindy.*)

CECILIA: Lindy, I didn't know—

LINDY: I was standing here. It makes no difference— I am interested in Captain Holworthy because I started his—his change. He's—he's rather a protégé of mine.
(*Enter Jeff.*)

CECILIA: I must go now. Mother is waiting for me—waiting luncheon.

MRS. D.: Will you stay and dine? (*Jeff coughs.*) We have not much to offer, but (*Jeff coughs*)—Jeff, will you be quiet!—but we would be so glad to have you.

CECILIA: No thank you, Mrs. Douglas. I think I'll be moving along. Good morning.

MRS. D.:
LINDY: } Good morning, Celia.

MRS. D.: Jeff, never do that again. Don't you know we are always glad to have anyone share whatever we have?

JEFF: Yassum, but we ain't got but one share. You can't share a share.

MRS. D.: That's true, but—

JEFF: Dey's plenty o' chairs— You don't have to chair de shares— I mean chair de chairs— No, I mean share de shares— Mrs. Douglas, luncheon is ready.

LINDY: The children?

MRS. D.: At the Taylors for luncheon.

LINDY: Oh, I almost forgot— Teacher—"that's me"—was presented with two oranges today. I'll get them.
(*Exit Lindy.*)

JEFF: (*Goes to window.*) Lawd o' massy! It's Mistah Charley!
(*Enter Captain Charles Douglas.*)

CHARLEY: Jeff!

MRS. D.: My boy!

CHARLEY: Mother!

JEFF: Large as life and twice as natural!

CHARLEY: Home at last, Mother. Where's Lindy?
(*Enter Lindy with plate of oranges. She sees Charley and drops plate which Jeff catches.*)

LINDY: Charley!

CHARLEY: Lindy! Home again. It seems great.

LINDY: And the war?

CHARLEY: Is over. Lee surrendered at Appomattox twelve hours ago. We did all we could— We were all gone— It was too much for us.

Mrs. D.: My poor boy!

Charley: I'm lucky to be alive and have a home to come back to, and a place for food. (*Looks at table.*)

Mrs. D.: Sit down. You must be famished.

Charley: Ah, milk! (*Drinks and sputters.*)

Mrs. D.: Why, what's the matter?

Charley: Nothing. But I've learned something.

Lindy: What?

Charley: There are some things worse than prison fare.

Mrs. D.: (*Drinks and sputters.*)

Lindy: (*Holds up glass.*) Jeff, what's the matter with this milk?

Jeff: (*Examines it carefully.*) Nothin'.

Charley: Nothing?

Mrs. D.: Nothing?

Lindy: Taste it!

Jeff: (*Tastes it.*) Oh, I recollect— I was enockomizing. Dey's water—a little bit—in dis milk— Jes' a bit.

Charley: I should say there was. Mother, are we in need of economizing like this?

Mrs. D.: Lindy teaches school.

Charley: By all that is holy! I'll get some work tonight. Mother, can you let me see exactly how we stand?

Mrs. D.: Yes, I have the accounts in the parlor.

(*Exit Mrs. Douglas, Captain Douglas and Jeff.*)

(*Enter Jim.*)

Jim: Good morning, Miss Lindy.

Lindy: Mr.—Captain Holworthy! Good morning.

Jim: It's—it's four years since I saw you last.

Lindy: Four years.

Jim: I was different then— I reckon we all were.

Lindy: Yes, I reckon we all were.

Jim: I've always thought that you rather set me right somehow.

Lindy: You do me great honor, Captain Holworthy.

Jim: I haven't forgotten it, either.

Lindy: You haven't?

Jim: No, I've—I've thought of it a lot more than you know. I realized long ago what I was.

Lindy: Well, you've come back different.

Jim: Yes, I reckon so. Do you remember the day when—when your brother was captured—what I said to you earlier in the day?

Lindy: Yes—yes, I think I do.

JIM: Well I—I can't explain but—it's you that I owe everything I've become—and that's not much, for the last soldier of a lost cause doesn't bring back much except an empty scabbard.

LINDY: And medals.

JIM: Medals.

LINDY: That little iron cross— Where did you get that?

JIM: Well, General Lee is the only one that can tell. He—he gives them away instead of cigars; he was out of cigars the day I called.

LINDY: I see you're more modest than you used to be.

JIM: It isn't much of a virtue when you have nothing to be vain about. My vanity wants satisfaction in another way now.

LINDY: Yes?

JIM: Yes. I could be proud—very proud if—Miss Lindy, you know what I want to say. You've been with me always. You made me go south. You have made me what I am. Whenever I received promotion it was because you inspired me. And—and—will you keep inspiring me?

LINDY: You ask me to be your wife?

JIM: Yes.

LINDY: Ji— Captain Holworthy, the man I marry must have my whole respect. I have lived in a war time and have had death and bravery brought very near to me. Bravery and moral courage are to me necessary to respect and love. I—I— Do you remember that morning you told me you had a strain somewhere in your nature of cowardice?

JIM: I remember.

LINDY: Tell me then, if you have completely conquered that?

JIM: And if I have.

LINDY: If you have, I—I will marry you.

JIM: Miss Lindy—Lindy, I am telling you the truth, though God only knows it hurts me to do it— I haven't conquered it. When it's something impulsive or where I don't have to reason, I've done many dangerous things, but when I think, I hesitate and give up. I got these trinkets for things like the first. This for a flag I took at Chickamauga, and this for saving Bragg from being shot at Shiloh; but I remember once when Lee asked for volunteers for secret service I didn't step out with the rest. And when I was in Libby prison before I was exchanged, three fellows who were with me had a chance to escape. They offered me an equal chance— It was an even chance—death or escape, and I didn't take it. I reckon it's a yellow streak in me somewhere. I would like to try once more.

LINDY: I see. But your chance of trying is over now.

JIM: I reckon.

LINDY: Well, goodbye Jim.

JIM: Goodbye Miss Lindy. You are right— I shouldn't have hoped for you. It was all a kind of a dream. (*Starts to go.*)

LINDY: You may have a chance yet to prove it.

JIM: No, I reckon not.

(*Exit Jim.*)

(*Enter Jeff.*)

JEFF: On celebration o' Mistah Charley's return kin ah get out de best tableclof? He's got a bit o' money and he's goin' to buy a good dinner.

LINDY: Yes Jeff, anything.

(*Exit Lindy.*)

JEFF: Now whah was dat? In—in de ole linen chest what hain't been used fo' yeahs. Lemme see. (*Goes to chest and opens it.*) Why I—I feels sumpin! (*Pulls out roll of money.*) Jumpin' Jerusalem it's money! Stacks of it! Northern money. Now dat's one hundred and one hundred is— Gee, I ain't no mathematician. Now lemme see— How did that money get thar? That chest ain't been used since Mistah Charley was captured out o' it three years ago. Why, don't I recollect he had some army money wit him? But it won't do to tell him it was dat— He'd send it away to General Lee. I'll—I'll—diplomatize—dat is, if I'm as good a liah as ah used to be. (*Steps heard outside. Starts sweeping.*)

(*Enter Mrs. Douglas and Charley.*)

JEFF: Mrs. Douglas, dere's a mattah ah wants to broach to you.

MRS. D.: What is it, Jeff?

JEFF: (*Hesitates and fumbles.*) On de later desease—demise of youh inflected husband he sum-mumoned me to his bedside jes aftah he died, and thrust into mah hands a small sum o' money which he said to give you after de triffic encountah which was den ragin' triumphantly and spasmodically—de very words he used—was done. De circumstances is now justified. Behold! (*Produces money.*)

CHARLEY: (*Takes it.*) Why, what's this?

MRS. D.: Why, I didn't know Arthur had any money when he died.

CHARLEY: Mother, it's twelve thousand dollars good money!
MRS. D.: If Jeff is telling the truth—
CHARLEY: Jeff?
JEFF: Mrs. Douglas, ma mouf is as clean from lyin' as is de grass from de snow—in de wintah time.
CHARLEY: It sounds true. Mother, we're rich! It's yours!
MRS. D.: It's too good to be true.
CHARLEY: And I'm off.
MRS. D.: Where?
CHARLEY: To see Cecilia.
(*Exit Charley.*)
JEFF: (*Aside.*) No sah, dere ain't nothin' like a little judicious lyin'!
(*Enter Lieutenant Percy Altwater.*)
PERCY: Mrs. Douglas, good morning. I fancy you are surprised to see me.
MRS. D.: I remember you perfectly, Mr. Hotwater.
PERCY: Altwater, my dear lady— Altwater.
MRS. D.: Excuse me.
PERCY: Certainly. Do you know, I hesitate to tell you why I returned. Do you know, I fancy Cupid has been at work and brought me back, fair as a—a— What am I fair as?
MRS. D.: A dancing elephant.
PERCY: Yes, a dancing elephant—er—oh, that doesn't sound just right, does it?
MRS. D.: Doesn't it, Mr. Warmwater?
PERCY: Altwater— Altwater.
MRS. D.: Excuse me.
PERCY: And as I was saying, I made the acquaintance of a most fascinating young lady at your house, Miss Virginia the tailor— I suppose they meant dressmaker. But even if the poor girl is a dressmaker, I would wave aside caste and er—marry her.
MRS. D.: Very condescending of you, Mr. Breakwater.
PERCY: Altwater— Altwater. I think so myself.
MRS. D.: But she isn't a dressmaker. That's just her name.
PERCY: Miss Virginia Dressmaker— That's a very odd name.
MRS. D.: No no!— Miss Virginia Taylor.
PERCY: Oh!
(*Enter Virginia.*)
VIRGINIA: Good morning, Mrs. Douglas.
MRS D.: Here is a friend of yours, Virginia.

VIRGINIA: Mr. Sweetwater!

PERCY: Miss Dressmaker!

(*Exit Mrs. Douglas.*)

VIRGINIA: I am delighted to see you again.

PERCY: Did you get my letter?

VIRGINIA: Yes, and the coat-of-arms.

PERCY: Rather a pretty crest, isn't it? I picked it up at a stationer's in Richmond.

VIRGINIA: Horrors!

PERCY: I'm sorry. You'll forgive me?

VIRGINIA: Yes. Who would not forgive the lost soldier of a last cause.

PERCY: Yes, but I'm not lost.

VIRGINIA: A slip of the tongue— I mean, the last soldier of a lost cause.

PERCY: Just so. It's rather sad.

VIRGINIA: Sad? It's all pathetic.

PERCY: Allopathic?

VIRGINIA: All pathetic.

PERCY: Miss Virginia, I've something to say to you.

VIRGINIA: It's coming!— Isn't it perfectly thirteenth century!

PERCY: Will you—will you—

VIRGINIA: Oh, I feel faint! Catch me! (*Fakes a faint.*) (*Percy springs forward.*) No, on the other side— It looks better. (*He helps her sink into chair.*) All right. Now go on.

PERCY: Will you marry me?

VIRGINIA: (*Dreaming.*) She looked tenderly into his dark brown eyes—

PERCY: But my eyes are not dark brown.

VIRGINIA: Sh!— And lisped—whispered tenderly—

PERCY: But this isn't a novel, you know.

VIRGINIA: Now you've spoiled the whole thing. I want to look back upon my proposal as something romantic.

PERCY: But this is my proposal. Will you—

VIRGINIA: (*Jumps up.*) Wait! It must be on bended knees in the flower garden, with the roses—

PERCY: And the bugs—

VIRGINIA: With the green grass—

PERCY: My poor trousers!

VIRGINIA: Come, Alphonso—

PERCY: But my name isn't Alphonso—

VIRGINIA: Never mind that— Come let us flit to the rose garden.
(*She flits, and Percy very awkwardly "flits" after her.*)
(*Percy and Virginia cease flitting.*)
(*Enter Angelina.*)

ANGELINA: Unchaperoned. This is perfectly awful. Unchaperoned!

PERCY: But we're engaged.

ANGELINA: How terrible! Blush, young lady, blush with shame. How could you admit it? I wouldn't admit it.

PERCY: You can't admit it unless you're engaged.

ANGELINA: Let me read you from this little work a short sermon on conduct of young ladies. "Young ladies should never under any conditions be alone with young men. The best authorities such as Miss Grayson, Miss Finch, Miss Spence and Miss Spindle agree in regard to this." (*Percy and Virginia have sneaked out.*) "A young lady on meeting a young man in the street should on no account—" (*Sees that the others are gone.*)

ANGELINA: Poor misguided people. I will pray for them. Yes I will pray for them. (*Exit.*)
(*Enter Lindy and two soldiers—Privates Willings and Barkis—from opposite doors.*)

LINDY: What do you want here?

PRIVATE W.: Good morning, lady.

PRIVATE B.: Greetings, fair one.

LINDY: Go out of here!

PRIVATE W.: We just came back from Appomattox, lady, and passing this spacious house, we thought perhaps you had a few trinkets to donate to the Union cause, just to cement the peace.
(*Removes cartridge belt and lays it on table.*)

LINDY: We have nothing, nothing in the house.

PRIVATE W.: We'll look and see, lady, if you have no objections.
(*Exit Privates Willings and Barkis.*)

LINDY: Jeff! Jeff! Oh, if Charley were only here.
(*Enter Jeff.*)

LINDY: Jeff, run out and find someone!— Any man!— Say that there are two Yankees here who are trying to pillage the house! Quick!
(*Exit Jeff.*)
(*Enter Private Barkis.*)

PRIVATE B.: Lady, where's the pantry?— I'm hungry. My pal prefers the valuables; I prefer the victuals. (*Lindy points toward pantry.*) I bid thee adieu. (*Bows low.*)

(*Exit Private Barkis.*)

(*Enter Private Willings.*)

PRIVATE W.: Lady, there ain't a valuable in the house— Not one! Except I see you've got a mighty fine necklace round your neck.

LINDY: Oh, you thief—you—!

(*Enter Jim Holworthy.*)

JIM: What's this?

LINDY: Jim, this man— (*Jim and Private Willings both rush to cartridge belt on table. Jim reaches it first. Willings fires twice with the two guns he is carrying but they refuse to work on account of lack of ammunition which Jim now holds.*)

JIM: I reckon I've got your stock of ammunition, Yank. You may go.

PRIVATE W.: Your lady friend here has a chain I want.

JIM: You may go, I say. (*Advances toward him.*)

PRIVATE W.: Keep back! I've got a friend in the kitchen.

JIM: I have many in the town. This lady has but to run out and—

PRIVATE W.: Can't we settle it peaceably? You don't want to get hurt by me and my friend, and we don't want to get chased by the town. But I've taken a fancy to that necklace. Isn't there any way we can decide?

JIM: Yes, there is a way—one way. (*Thinks.*) Are we at truce for a minute.

PRIVATE W.: Yes.

JIM: Load one of these pistols.

PRIVATE W.: One?

JIM: Yes. Now the lady will take them both, mix them up behind her back, then she'll put one in each hand, and you choose one. I'll take the other. Then we fire. One will refuse to work.

PRIVATE W.: My God! Only one pistol loaded? But the lady—

JIM: You may trust the lady. May he not, Lindy?

LINDY: Yes. But I didn't mean for you to do this, Jim!

JIM: It will end it one way or the other.

PRIVATE W.: Here they are. (*Hands his two pistols to Lindy who mixes them as directed.*)

JIM: All right, Yank— Choose.

PRIVATE W.: I—I—oh, I'm going, Reb— I can stand a battle, but you've got some nerve.
(*Exit Private Willings.*)

JIM: (*Pause.*) Well, I reckon I bluffed him. Glad to have been of service to you. Goodbye.

LINDY: You're not going, Jim?

JIM: Yes.

LINDY: And you have nothing to say?

JIM: Nothing, I reckon. What's the use?

LINDY: I think, Jim, you have had your chance.

JIM: Then you think you really will—?

LINDY: Jim, come here— You are a worse coward than you were four years ago.
(*They embrace.*)

(*Quick Curtain.*)

END OF SECOND ACT AND PLAY

Assorted Spirits

Two men dressed in similar devils' costumes—one bent on getting a bargain by haunting a house, the other there accidentally because of a confusion of addresses—and a female burglar who uses the name of the well-known contemporary actress, Minnie Maddern Fiske, and swipes the ten thousand dollars brought to purchase the house and later returns, this time imitating a book agent, were only some of those involved in the wildly improbable circumstances here. This purposeful mix-up of people and places, of course, was nothing new to Fitzgerald. In *A Regular Fix,* that very first Elizabethan Dramatic Club production in which he had participated, the hero wakes up in a strange house after getting drunk the previous night and is forced to take on a new identity. And, of course, both Tony Gonzoles of *The Girl from Lazy J* and Thorton Hart Dudley of *The Captured Shadow* had assumed deceptive poses. In addition, Fitzgerald also included in *Assorted Spirits* another of his early femmes fatales, this time Clara King of Missouri, who smokes despite the conventions of the day, stays up late, has been engaged three times, and is wooed unsuccessfully by the delicate, hay-fever suffering Dickie Wetherby. Contrasting with this pursuit are two others, the more conventional though hardly more believable courtship of Cecile Wetherby and William Chapman as well as the renewal of an old relationship between Madame Zada, the fortune teller, and Josephus Hendrix, the house haunter. The plot was overly complicated. Yet because of the many humorous situations, the audiences at the Y.W.C.A. auditorium and at White Bear Yacht Club reacted with great enthusiasm to Fitzgerald's last Elizabethan Dramatic Club play.

Assorted Spirits

A two act farce written for
The Elizabethan Dramatic Club
by Francis Scott Fitzgerald

Presented at the Y.W.C.A. Auditorium and the White Bear Yacht Club on Tuesday and Wednesday evenings,
September 8 and 9, 1914
Under the Direction of Elizabeth Magoffin.

CAST OF CHARACTERS

WILLIAM CHAPMAN, *gentleman spirit*	Gustave Schurmeier
JOSEPHUS HENDRIX, *gentleman spirit*	John L. Mitchell
PETER WETHERBY, *who needs $10,000*	Scott Fitzgerald
DICKIE WETHERBY, *a hypochondriac with hay fever*	James Armstrong
MULLIGAN } *Policemen*	McNeil Seymore
O'FLARITY } *Policemen*	Robert Clark
CECILE WETHERBY, *in love with Will*	Eleanor Alair
CLARA KING, *from Missouri*	Katherine Schulze
SECOND STORY SALLE	Dorothy Greene
MADAME ZADA, *a fortune teller*	Alice Lyon
MISS SPIGOT, *doting aunt of Will*	Margaret Armstrong
HULDA, *a maid, from Sweden*	Betty Mudge

Act I—*The Wetherby Home—9:30 P. M.*
Act II—*Same—Next morning*

Furnishings—*up-to-date living room, two closets in evidence.*
Costumes—*Modern. Two devils' suits. Two policeman uniforms.*

Assorted Spirits

ACT I

(*Curtain rises showing Cecile and Miss Spigot in conversation.*)

MISS S.: My dear Cecile, I have had such a busy day.

CEC.: You have?

MISS S.: Yes, you know my nephew William is coming home tomorrow.

CEC.: How perfectly delightful; I haven't seen him for three years.

MISS S.: He has been very successful in the railroad business.

CEC.: So?

MISS S.: His business is contracting.

CEC.: How interesting. Contracting and expanding, I suppose.

MISS S.: (*Indignantly.*) He is not a contortionist, he is a railroad contractor.

CEC.: I see.

MISS S.: I suppose all the young girls in the vicinity will be angling for him.

CEC.: Yes, no doubt.

MISS S.: However, I have no one in mind; yet do you know I have always fancied that you and he would make a beautiful match.

CEC.: Miss Spigot!

MISS S.: My dear, my dear, you must control yourself. As an old friend of the family—

CEC.: (*Interrupting.*) Still, I want you to know that I am distinctly not angling for him.

(*Dick looks in at door.*)

MISS S.: Of course, of course. William is in town now.

CEC.: I am glad to hear it.

MISS S.: I haven't seen him yet. He is going to a fancy dress ball tonight and he is dressing at his club. I expect him before midnight.

CEC.: (*Yawns.*) You must tell him to call.

MISS S.: Oh yes, he is the most—

DICK: (*Outside.*) Oh Hulda, you had better close all the windows, it is going to rain in a few minutes.

MISS S.: (*Rising hurriedly.*) Well, I must be going.

CEC.: So sorry, come again some time.

(*They both go out at left.*)

(*Dickie sticks his head around the corner and slowly comes into the room. Re-enter Cecile.*)

DICK: Is she gone, Sis? (*Feels pulse.*)

CEC.: (*Sinks into chair.*) Yes, thank Heaven.

DICK: I thought that would get her.

CEC.: What do you mean, isn't it going to rain?

DICK: Not a cloud in the sky, but I was so nervous! And my hay fever starts tomorrow.

CEC.: I thought she would never stop, and the worst of it is she has her eyes on Dad. She was telling me about her nephew who is coming home tonight.

DICK: What, Will Chapman coming home tonight? That's good.

CEC.: I haven't seen him since he went away three years ago. He has been quite successful, I believe, a railroad contractor.

DICK: Well, I hope he hasn't turned out like his aunt—the old bore. I like brilliant women.

CEC.: What is your idea of a brilliant woman?

DICK: Every widow between thirty-five and forty-five who has no children and doesn't wear glasses.

CEC.: Miss Spigot shows unlimited nerve. She copied her house after ours and there *she* is at 225 Greenwood Place and we're at 225 Greenbriar Street. It's a wonder more people haven't already gotten mixed up. We get her letters continually.

(*Enter Mr. Wetherby.*)

MR. W.: (*Gruffly.*) Well, I found a purchaser for the house.

DICK: Thank heavens, Father, then we can live less economically.

MR. W.: If you had gone to work we'd have done that long ago. The only thing you are fit for is signing patent medicine testimonials. You want a position where you can dress expensively, cultivate an English accent and babble about art. (*Sits down in chair and picks up newspaper.*)

DICK: (*Enthusiastically.*) Just the thing!

MR. W.: Well, I'll set you up as an interior decorator. Why, you've got a suit for every day in the year.

DICK: Yes, this is it. (*Pointing to suit he is wearing.*) If I wasn't so delicate. I've got a play now in mind. I'll write it up next week if I feel well enough.

CEC.: Who is going to buy the house?

MR. W.: Hm, hm.

CEC.: Who is going to buy it, Dad?

MR. W.: Can't I read the paper in peace?

CEC.: Who is going to buy it?

MR. W.: Buy what? Oh yes, why I got a letter today from Josephus Hendrix, a second cousin of mine. Haven't seen him for years. He says he wants to buy it, but he makes a blamed queer stipulation.

CEC.: What's the stipulation?

MR. W.: What's what? Oh, he says the house is haunted.

CEC.: }
DICK: } Haunted!

MR. W.: Yes. So Cousin Josephus and his ward, Miss Clara King, will come tomorrow morning to spend a few days. Then if the house proves all right he'll buy it.

DICK: Miss Clara King—age, please.

MR. W.: How should I know?

DICK: What do you think?

MR. W.: How should I think?

DICK: Oh, like everyone else thinks.

MR. W.: Oh, she's seventeen, I suppose.

DICK: Oh, a young kid. Light or dark?

MR. W.: I am sure I don't know. Why the de—

CEC.: Tut, tut, papa, you must not use profane language.

MR. W.: I will use any language I want to.

(*The telephone rings. Enter Hulda, who goes to the phone.*)

HULDA: Hello—what's that—I tank so—aw, this is me. (*Sits down.*) Oh, Mr. Wetherby, yes, he's here—nothing is the matter with me, how are you? Oh, he bane fine. Yes I will get him.

MR. W.: Who are you talking to?

HULDA: There is a man wants to speak to you.

MR. W.: (*Goes to the phone.*) Hello —yes—yes—oh, that was that damned Swede girl. Yes, why Cousin Josephus, I didn't expect you till tomorrow —yes— well—you will be up in fifteen minutes. Goodbye. (*Rings off. To children.*) Cousin Joseph has arrived unexpectedly. He and his ward are at the station now. See to their rooms—we have got to make a good impression.

CEC.: Very well, Father.

DICK: I can't make beds with my weak back.

(*Exit Dick and Cecile. Mr. W. sits down and picks up newspaper. Bell rings. Enter Hulda, running.*)

MR. W.: (*Testily.*) What's your name?

HULDA: Oh, I answer to "Hey" or any loud cry.

Mr. W.: What are you always running through the house for? Don't you ever sit still?

Hulda: To answer the bell.

Mr. W.: Answer who?

Hulda: The bell—

Mr. W.: What bell?

Hulda: The door bell—

Mr. W.: Well answer it and don't stand here talking.

(*Exit Hulda, Mr. W. picks up paper, re-enter Hulda with card on plate.*)

Hulda: Lady to see you sir.

Mr. W.: A lady, what lady? Does she want me?

Hulda: Oh yes, she sayd you sant for her.

Mr. W.: Oh yes, I remember.

Hulda: Who is she? I can't read the card.

Mr. W.: Never you mind who she is. Show her in. (*Takes card, exit Hulda.*)

Mr. W.: (*Reading from card.*) Madame Zada, fortune teller, astrologer, mind reader—hm, humbug!

(*Enter Hulda followed by Madame Zada, who advances toward Mr. W. Exit Hulda.*)

Mme.: Well, Brother Peter.

Mr. W.: Sh—sh—

Mme.: What's the matter, are you ashamed of me?

Mr. W.: Not exactly, but if my children should know that my sister and their aunt was a fortune teller—

Mme.: Well, I must earn my living. Since my husband's desertion I have tried everything. I went back to my old profession of manicuring but I have lost the knack and there is money in fortune telling.

Mr. W.: Well, here is why I sent for you. I have a prospective buyer for my house but he says that he has heard it is haunted.

Mme.: Well, where do I come in?

Mr. W.: Hold your horses. I want to ask you first if you think there is anything in spirits.

Mme.: Well, they are all very well in moderation.

Mr. W.: What do you mean?

Mme.: Of course I am not a drinking woman myself, but—

Mr. W.: No, no, I mean ghosts.

MME.: Ghosts?

MR. W.: Do you believe in them?

MME.: If there is money in it.

MR. W.: Well if there should be by any chance a ghost in this house do you think you could argue with it with your second sight—er—persuade it to shift its base of operations, discourage it, give it a cash bonus—anything to get rid of it. I can't afford to have a ghost around here.

MME.: Is it violent?

MR. W.: How should I know, do you think I wrestle with it?

MME.: You want me to make sure if there is one?

MR. W.: Exactly. I want you to stay in the house tonight. I am sure the ghost would be open to an agreement of some kind.

MME.: No doubt, no doubt, and what would I get?

MR. W.: Money, money, everybody wants it. I wish it was all in Hades.

MME.: Peter, I see you are still profane. Some day you will have an apparition or something and that will cure you.

MR. W.: Well, be sure I'll fully recompense you. Is it a bargain?

MME.: Very well.

MR. W.: We will go to my study to arrange the details of the hunt. (*They go out—the bell rings. Hulda shows in Josephus and Clara. Cecile and Dickie enter from the opposite side.*)

DICK: Ah, Mr. Hendrix and Miss King!

CEC.: Cousin Josephus!

CLARA: How do you do, Mr. Wetherby and Miss Wetherby, I suppose?

JO.: Ah, good evening, good evening! Tee hee, your father, eh, where is the sly old fox?

DICK: Let us show you to your rooms first, you must be tired. This way, sir.

(*They all go out left.*)

(*Enter William Chapman. He wears an overcoat and a slouch hat.*)

WILL: (*Calls.*) Auntie, oh, Miss Spigot. (*Takes off his coat and hat, disclosing a devil suit such as those worn at masquerades.*) Well that was the slowest dance and I felt like a fool in this costume. (*Sits down.*) Oh, it's good to be home. I wonder where Auntie is.

(*Enter Hulda.*)

Oh, just tell your mistress I am here.

(*Hulda screams and rushes out.*)

Well, I'll be darned. Is the woman crazy? I wonder where I could get a drink of water. I think I'll explore.

(*Exit on left. Enter Hulda from right. She turns on the light.*)

HULDA: Well, for the love of St. Olaf, I must have been dreaming. I bane thought I saw Old Nick himself. Oh, my heart's beating like when Ole kissed me last night. What's this? Mr. Wetherby's hat and coat. I'll take them to his room.

(*Picks up Will's hat and coat and goes out. Enter Will.*)

WILL: Hello, someone turned the lights on. I wonder where my aunt is. This looks strange. Why, what's this picture, and this, and where are all the old ones? (*Walks around.*) Why this doesn't look familiar. I wonder if it could be the wrong house. No, the cabby told me this was 225 Greenbriar Street. Let's see if I have the address right. (*Takes card from pocket.*) What—what—what—225 Greenwood Place? Good Heavens, I am in the wrong house. (*Looks around frantically.*) Where is that coat? Oh Lord, it's gone, and me in this costume. I say, I must find my coat.

(*Exit on left. Enter Clara and Josephus on right.*)

JO.: Well, Clara, how do you like the house?

CLARA: Oh, it's so so. But I don't see that it's any better than the one we have now, unless you want more room.

JO.: (*Not hearing.*) Hey?

CLARA: I say unless you want room.

JO.: Wash room? Where, I don't see it.

CLARA: No I say, why do you want this house?

JO.: Ah yes, well I'll tell you a secret. The Red Wing, Stillwater and Minneapolis Railroad Company are going to put a spur through here, and they will have to buy this property. I thought if I could get the house cheap it would be a good investment to snap it up quick.

CLARA: Why, I don't think that is a bit nice.

JO.: Hey?

CLARA: I say that isn't very nice.

JO.: Ah yes, yes, it is very nice. And that isn't all. If I can prove that the house is haunted it will greatly decrease its value and I can insist on a very low price.

CLARA: What do you mean?

JO.: Simply this— I went to a costumer yesterday and bought a devil suit, red cloth with horns and all, you know. While I am here I shall prowl around in this suit and let some of the people see me. Then I'll insist the house is haunted. He! He!

CLARA: Why, this is criminal, I won't allow it.

JO.: You must remember you are my ward.

CLARA: Well, please do not cheat these people.

JO.: Tut, tut, child I—

(*Enter Mr. Wetherby.*)

MR. W.: Well, Cousin Josephus, how are you, stingy as ever?

JO.: Hey, Cousin Peter?

MR. W.: I say, are you stingy as ever?

JO.: I don't quite hear you.

MR. W.: I see you don't.

JO.: Hey? Oh yes, this is my ward, Miss Clara King.

MR. W.: How de do, Miss King.

CLARA: How do you do.

(*Enter Dickie.*)

MR. W.: (*To Jo.*) And now you and I can go in the library and talk business, Cousin Josephus.

JO.: Surely, ah—

MR. W.: (*Crossing to Dickie.*) Amuse little Miss King, won't you, Dickie?

DICK: (*Dejectedly.*) I suppose I'll have to.

(*Exit Wetherby and Josephus.*)

DICK: (*Crossing to Clara, patronizingly.*) Hello, Clara.

CLARA: Hello—Dickie.

DICK: (*Taken back.*) How are—are you?

CLARA: I am quite well, thank you. How are you?

DICK: I'm never very well but I'm as well as one can expect; then one's hay-fever comes on tomorrow. Ah, you live in St. Joseph, Missouri, don't you?

CLARA: Yes.

DICK: How long have you lived in the United States?

CLARA: Sir!

DICK: I beg your pardon. It slipped out. (*Aside.*) How shall I amuse her? (*To Clara.*) I suppose you must have awfully good times there with your—ah, little playmates?

CLARA: (*Carelessly.*) Yes, we manage to scare up sufficient amusement. I suppose you have fun here playing baseball and football with the other boys?

DICK: Ah yes, I fancy I am a little beyond that now, but I—er—used to, before my health took a turn—and all that.

CLARA: Ah, you used to? Since you put on long trousers, I suppose?

DICK: (*Changing the subject hurriedly.*) Would you like some lemonade, er—Clara, Miss Clara?

CLARA: No, thank you.

DICK: Some cake or candy?

CLARA: No, but (*confidentially*) have you a cigaret?

DICK: (*Startled.*) Ha, er (*looks around and draws chair closer*). Where did you say you lived?

CLARA: St. Joseph.

DICK: And they say Missouri is slow. I am sorry I have no cigarets with me and I don't allow anyone to smoke my pipe. Shall I get you a cigar?

CLARA: No, don't bother. I had a cigaret at the depot and I have some in my room.

DICK: Whew!

CLARA: What did you say?

DICK: I said that is a pretty brooch you have on.

CLARA: It ought to be, I traded in three engagement rings for it. It got me in more trouble—

(*Enter Wetherby and Josephus from right.*)

(*Enter Hulda from left.*)

MR. W.: Well, then if the house proves unhaunted you give me ten thousand for it.

JO.: Yes, I have it right here and otherwise— (*Shrugs his shoulders.*) I'll entrust it to your son for safekeeping—

MR. W.: Come, Dickie, and show Mr. Hendrix to his room.

(*Wetherby and Hendrix go out. Clara goes to door.*)

CLARA: Ta, ta, Dickie.

DICK: Good evening, Miss King. (*Exit Clara.*)

A beautiful girl in the house and my hay-fever starts tomorrow.

(*Dickie shakes his head and goes out.*)

(*Window slowly opens.*)

(*Enter Second Story Salle—whistles.*)

(*Enter Hulda.*)

S. S. S.: Hello?

HULDA: I guess I left the window open all right?

S. S. S.: Yes. Well, what's the dope?

HULDA: There's a gentleman visiting here who has given ten thousand dollars to Mr. Dickie to keep for him.

S. S. S.: Ten thousand dollars?

HULDA: Yes.

S. S. S.: And who has it?

HULDA: Mr. Dickie.

S. S. S.: Where's the young fellow's room?

HULDA: Head of stairs on the left.

S. S. S.: I'll remember.

HULDA: And for the love of Christina! be careful! The house is full—a—people!

S. S. S.: It'll take more than a house full of people to catch Second Story Salle!

HULDA: And where do I come in?

S. S. S.: You do what I tell you, and keep your mouth tight. And I'll come here tomorrow morning dressed as a book agent and give you your share.

HULDA: All right but be awful careful.

(*Exit Hulda and S. S. S.*)

(*Enter Will.*)

WILL: Whoever took that overcoat took it far away. What am I going to do? Oh—

(*Enter Cecile.*)

CEC.: Hello.

WILL: How do you do. Pardon me, madam, permit me to introduce myself.

CEC.: Don't bother, I recognize you.

WILL: Oh, you do? Well, you have the advantage of me.

CEC.: My name is Ce-ce-cile Wether-b-by.

WILL: O yes, no wonder you know me.

CEC.: Sir!

WILL: You ought to, I used to play with you as a child.

CEC.: Sir, I admit I was a tomboy but I never entered into any communication with you.

WILL: But my dear young lady!

CEC.: I am not your dear young lady.

WILL: Perhaps I am not as fierce as I look.

CEC.: Were I not a lady I would tell you in plain language to go home.

WILL: You have told me, as far as I can see.

CEC.: I don't see you going.

WILL: I want to explain first. I came here quite by accident. I was looking for Miss Spigot.

CEC.: Allow me to congratulate you, I expected as much.

WILL: You remember she is a relation of mine.

CEC.: I don't doubt it.

WILL: And I was going to her house when here I am by accident in yours. I can't get out for my overcoat has disappeared and I am too—

CEC.: (*Interrupting.*) Natural for safety.

WILL: And the worst of it is that you seem to have forgotten your old playmate Will Chapman.

CEC.: Will Chapman?

WILL: Surely.

CEC.: I had not heard of your demise. Believe me, I am very sorry.

WILL: Why, what do you mean? Oh heavens—what—what—you thought—oh Lord—this is too much! Come here and pinch me, I am real flesh and blood.

CEC.: Oh, I thought for a minute—

WILL: That I was— I know I shouldn't have worn this costume. It looks like the de—

CEC.: Where did you get it?

WILL: I wore it to a masquerade ball.

CEC.: Oh, I see. But how did you get *here*?

WILL: I got here by accident and now I can't get out, for someone took my overcoat.

CEC.: Well, listen. You must not be seen by anyone here. A man is here who wants to buy the house, but he won't if he thinks the house is haunted. You must hide in this closet. (*Goes to closet on left and throws open the door.*) In about half an hour, when everyone is asleep, you come upstairs and I will leave an overcoat for you in the front hall.

WILL: Thank you, Cecile— I am—

CEC.: Now get in there and be quiet!

(*He goes in closet, she shuts door, turns out lights and exits.*)
(*Enter Josephus with false mustache and goatee in his hand. He is dressed in a devil's suit like Will's. He turns up lights.*)

JO.: (*Looking anxiously behind him.*) That's funny, I'm all in a tremor. I could have sworn a minute ago that I saw my wife, my Amelia that I left so many years ago. I must have been dreaming. And now to frighten a few people. Te, he, he!
(*Enter Clara.*)

CLARA: Uncle Josephus!

JO.: What are you doing up at this hour?

CLARA: Listen, you must not do this. It is perfectly terrible. Some-one might shoot you.

JO.: Nonsense, child, I can not afford to pay ten thousand dollars for the house.

CLARA: You are cheating Mr. Wetherby.

JO.: Tut, tut, cheating is a bad word.

CLARA: Listen, there is someone coming. Quick, you must hide. Look, quick in here.

(*She opens the other closet and puts him in. She goes out quickly at right. Enter Cecile, from left.*)

CEC.: It's rather mean, but I can't take any chances. I must lock Will in until everyone is asleep. Let's see, where did I put him? Oh yes, in this closet. (*Goes to closet where Josephus is and locks door. There is pounding on the inside.*) It's too bad, Will, but I've got to do it.

(*Exit Cecile, turning out lights.*)

(*Enter Second Story Salle at left.*)

(*Enter Dick at right.*)

DICK: Good evening.

S. S. S.: Ah, good evening!

DICK: May I ask what you want here?

S. S. S.: Certainly— You may ask.

DICK: Well, what—er do you want?

S. S. S.: Didn't you get my card?

DICK: No.

S.S.S.: That's strange; I told the maid to take it to— Ah, you are Mr. Richard Wetherby, I presume?

DICK: Yes.

S. S. S.: Well, you're the one I want to see.

DICK: Yes, yes, I see—but why?

S. S. S.: Well, you see it's this way— I've heard of you—

DICK: No doubt.

S. S. S.: As a playwright.

DICK: You have? Ah, won't you have a seat?

S. S. S.: (*Taking chair.*)You have probably heard of me—

DICK: Yes, yes.

S. S. S.: My name is—Minnie Maddern Fiske.

DICK: Oh yes yes; have another seat— Have a cigar— I mean er—

S. S. S.: No doubt you catch my drift, or shall I snow again?

DICK: Ah yes,—that is—er—

S. S. S.: As a fellow professional, I took the liberty of dropping in at this unconventional hour—

DICK: Don't mention it.

S. S. S.: To see about your er—play—"The Dappled Dawn."

DICK: Ah yes, but it's in a very primitive state; scarcely more than a title, to tell the truth.

S. S. S.: Never tell the truth; it is a confession of failure, a sign that your imagination is exhausted.

DICK: Yes of course. But about the play of mine— —

S. S. S.: I want it. (*Takes ten thousand dollars from Dick's pocket.*) —(*Aside.*)—And I have it!

DICK: Mrs. Fiske— May I call you Minnie?— You may have it.

S. S. S.: Tomorrow I would like to discuss it with you. We can fix a date for then, not for tonight; we artists have our trials, you know—temperament and—

DICK: Hay fever! Yes, yes.

S. S. S.: (*Starting to faint— Hand grasping ten thousand dollars behind her.*) Oh, I am going to faint! My head is swimming—Water!

DICK: (*As he exits.*) Water for Mrs. Fiske!! (*Exit r.*)

(*S. S. S. sees Will peep out of closet, screams, drops banknotes and jumps out of window.*)

(*Enter Hulda, she picks up money.*)

HULDA: What's this? *The* ten thousand dollars. Second Story Salle must have dropped it. (*Exit.*)

(*Enter Dick r. with glass of water.*)

DICK: Mrs. Fiske! Mrs. Fiske! Why, she's gone!— But ah!—Mrs. Fiske in "The Dappled Dawn," by Richard Cartridgebelt Wetherby. Soon I'll have a wad the size of—(*feels pocket and finds ten thousand dollars gone*). Good Lord, it's gone. (*Drops glass of water.*) Someone's taken that ten thousand dollars! What a mess I'm in. I mustn't let anyone know. I'll—I'll search the house. (*Exit in a rush.*)

(*Enter Mr. Wetherby and Mme. Zada, carrying candles.*)

MR. W.: Sh! The people upstairs mustn't hear us.

MME.: This sort of thing always makes me nervous. I have almost forgotten the formula for confronting spirits. Let's see. (*Produces book.*) Question—whence do you come? Answer, from the land whence none return. Question—where do you go? Answer—to pace the night alone. Question—what do you wish from me? Answer—

Jo.: (*In closet.*) Let me out of here.

Mr. W.: What was that?

Mme.: What, I didn't hear anything.

Mr. W.: I must have been mistaken.

Mme.: Let me see, where was I? Question—why do you weep? Answer—

Jo.: (*In closet.*) I am boiling to death.

Mr. W.: I distinctly heard something then.

Mme.: Yes, a hollow, muffled voice.

Mr. W.: It's the ghost!

Mme.: Walk around the room and see.

Mr. W.: Round the room, pshaw, what would I do walking around the room? Spose he cut me open on a new carpet. The idea! You must be crazy. Walk around yourself.

Mme.: I have a sore foot. (*Knocking is heard.*)

Mr. W.: Go, let him in.

Mme.: You fool, it's spirit knocking. (*Three knocks.*) Three knocks, that's D. (*Three more knocks.*) Three more knocks—that's D again. (*Three more knocks.*) Three D's—let's see, d—d—d—what can it mean?

Mr. W.: Probably he stuttered when he was on earth.

Mme.: Listen, I will go in your study and wait. You stay here and if anything happens call me.

Mr. W.: Er, you think we had best separate? The ghost might overpower you.

Mme.: Are you frightened?

Mr. W.: No. no.

Mme.: Well, stay here. (*Exit Madame Z.*)

Mr. W.: (*Sitting down.*) Whew, this is tiresome business.

(*Enter Clara, silently. She goes to Josephus's closet silently and tries door.*)

Clara: Locked! What shall I do? He will have to stay there till morning.

(*Exit Clara. Mr. W. has fallen asleep. The music starts playing "He's a Devil." The door of the left hand closet opens slowly and Will steals softly out. He tips over a chair.*)

WILL: Dash it!

MR. W.: (*Waking up.*) What the devil!

WILL: (*Coming forward.*) How do you do, Mr. Wetherby?

MR. W.: Oh Lord, oh Heavens, I'll never curse again! Never as I live, I swear it. Oh sir, go way and leave me.

WILL: You are a hospitable lot, I must say. When people come to see me I am more hospitable.

MR. W.: Yes, I know you are.

WILL: Come to my home in the future and see.

MR. W.: (*Groaning.*) Never, never.

(*Mme. Z. has stolen softly in.*)

MME.: Throw up your hands.

WILL: Why? (*Puts up hands.*)

MR. W.: A pistol does no good—you can't hurt him with a bullet.

MME.: Why, he's real flesh and blood. He's no more devil than I am.

MR. W.: That doesn't mean anything.

MME.: Pinch him and see.

MR. W.: I don't want to pinch him. Pinch him yourself. Then you are not a devil?

WILL: No.

MR. W.: Then how dare you come in my house?

WILL: Don't you allow anyone but devils in your house?

MME.: Here, hold this pistol pointed at him while I call up the police.

(*Mr. W. takes pistol.*)

WILL: The police!

MME.: (*Picking up receiver.*) Central, give me the police station, quick. Yes.

WILL: The police, oh Lord! (*To Mr. W.*) Sir, since you insist on thinking that I am not human I will prove to you that I am. I can pick up things like this snuffer (*picks snuffer from candle-stick*) and use it—

(*Snuffs out candle, plunging room into darkness. Mr. W. fires pistol. Mme. screams, they search for light. It flashes on, showing Hulda, Cecile and Clara in doorway.*)

MR. W.: I've got him. (*Wrestles with Dickie.*)

ALL: What's the matter?

MR. W.: There are spirits in here.

MME.: Spirits of ammonia—it was a man!

CECILE:
CLARA: } (*Aside.*) How did he get out?

DICK: (*Aside.*)No, I fear it was a woman—(*To others.*) Let's search for him.

(*They search.*)

HULDA: He bane not here.

MR. W.: Let's search the whole downstairs.

(*They all go out. The music starts playing "He's a Devil" and Will sticks his head out from under the table. S. S. S. sticks her head in the window.*)

S. S. S.: Well, Mr. Satan, I'll just take that ten thousand dollars.

(*Curtain.*)

ACT II

(*Breakfast table laid as curtain rises. Doorbell rings. Hulda answers it. Enter Hulda followed by Miss Spigot.*)

MISS S.: So the family's not up yet?

HULDA: No ma'am, I thought they was going to stay up the whole night.

MISS S.: It doesn't surprise me. What was the matter?

HULDA: Spirits.

MISS S.: Spirits?

HULDA: Yes, and lots of them.

MISS S.: Shocking! Shocking! And who were the er—inebriates?

HULDA: The which?

MISS S.: The victims.

HULDA: Well, there was Mr. Wetherby.

MISS S.: Was he very much ah—

HULDA: Terrible—he couldn't sleep all night.

MISS S.: And who else?

HULDA: Well, there was a strange lady—she was very bad.

MISS S.: Oh, a strange lady? There are more skeletons in the family closet.

(*Will sticks his head out of closet and quickly withdraws it.*)

HULDA: Well you just take it from me— I was feeling very queer myself, ma'am.

MISS S.: You wicked girl!

HULDA: I couldn't help it.

MISS S.: They forced it on you, I suppose. What a den of perfidy!

HULDA: Yes'm, I'd just said goodbye to Ole—he's my steady—on the back porch when I hears screamin' and carryin' on, and when I went in they all started looking for the spirits.

MISS S.: Where were they?

HULDA: Vanished.

MISS S.: I'll wager you could account for some of them.

HULDA: It was two o'clock before they quieted down.

MISS S.: And while they were here with their spirits and carousals I was at home praying for my nephew.

HULDA: Your nevy?

MISS S.: Yes, he hasn't come home yet. That's why I came over—to see if Mr. Dick has heard from him. Poor boy! Something awful must have happened.

HULDA: Yes'm, he's probably dead (*looks carelessly at table*) or else in a penitentiary.

MISS S.: No such thing.

HULDA: You never can tell—my Ole—

MISS S.: Bother your Ole!

HULDA: My Ole's a fine fellow, I tell you.

(*Enter Cecile.*)

CEC.: Good morning, Miss Spigot.

MISS S.: I'm *sure* I wish you a *very* good morning.

CEC.: What's wrong?

MISS S.: Nothing—nothing of *consequence.* Don't bother, *Miss* Wetherby, you must be worn out.

CEC.: Oh, Hulda has told you of our little affair with the spirits? (*Laughs.*)

MISS S.: She has, indeed, and pardon me if I say that I see no cause for laughing.

CEC.: Well, it *was* rather funny.

MISS S.: I came to see Mr. Dickie about something.

CEC.: He isn't down yet.

MISS S.: I shall wait in the library. (*Exit.*)

(*Enter Mr. W.*)

MR. W.: Hm—hm—

CEC.: Good morning, Father.

MR. W.: Where's the paper?

CEC.: It hasn't been brought in yet.

MR. W.: Tell that Swede to get it. Tell her to hurry. Got anything fit to eat for breakfast?

(*Exit Hulda.*)

MR. W.: Well, it's lucky Cousin Josephus slept through all that turmoil.

CEC.: He hasn't come down yet.

MR. W.: Because I've got to have ten thousand before tomorrow morning to keep my business above water.

(*Hulda enters and leaves paper for Mr. W.*)

MR. W.: (*Not seeing it.*) Where's that paper?

HULDA: Right there.

MR. W.: Where?

CEC.: There.

MR. W.: Well, don't stand here staring like an idiot—get me my breakfast.

CEC.: Excuse me Father. (*She goes silently to door of left hand wardrobe—tries it.*) How did he get out? It's still locked. I may as well unlock it. (*She does so and then goes out. Hulda comes in and puts toast and coffee down by Mr. W. Exit.*)

MR. W.: Isn't she ever going to bring that breakfast? (*Gets up and goes into kitchen. Will comes out of closet, gets toast and coffee and goes back. Enter Hulda and Mr. W.*)

HULDA: I just brought you some.

MR. W.: You didn't bring me any. If you did where is it?

HULDA: I bane tank it's the spirits!

MR. W.: Spirits be damned! You didn't bring it in!

HULDA: Well I'll get another cup. (*He sits down grumbling. She goes out, returns with another cup and exits.*)

MR. W.: Where's my toast? I don't want coffee without toast. (*Goes out toward kitchen. Josephus comes out of closet, gets coffee and goes back again.*)

MR. W.: (*Coming in.*) Well hurry up with it. Where's my coffee? (*Searches in pockets.*) What took that coffee? (*Goes to door.*) Hulda, I want more coffee. Someone's taken my coffee. (*Takes up paper, grumbling.*)

(*Enter Dickie.*)

MR. W.: It's about time you were down stairs— Well, why don't you answer? Don't sit there like an idiot. What's the matter?

DICK: By hay-fever's cob.

MR. W.: Your what?

DICK: By hay-fever. I couldn't sleep a wick last dight.

MR. W.: Who expected you to sleep a week in one night?

DICK: Oh, I dot expect ady sypathy. I cad breathe through by dose.

MR. W.: Well, breathe through your ears.

DICK: Ad that's dot the worst.

MR. W.: What's the matter now?

DICK: You dow that ted thousad dollars that Mr. Hendricks idtrusted be with last dight?

MR. W.: Yes.

DICK: Well, it's god!

MR. W.: Gone?

DICK: Vadished. I wed up idto by roob ad looked in the drawer where I'd left it, ad it was gone.

MR. W.: What a mess! That fellow last night must have taken it. This is the limit! Have you telephoned the police?

DICK: Yes.

MR. W.: Well, the only thing for you to do is to marry Miss King. I hear she's an heiress. Otherwise there's the deuce to pay.

DICK: I like the way you dispose of be. But I know she has her eyes od be, and she's dot the first one.

MR. W.: Well, propose to her. That's our only chance. You always were a bonehead. I've got to have that money by twelve o'clock to keep my business from going to smash.

DICK: Is it as bad as that?

MR. W.: It certainly is.

DICK: Well, id by dervous codition I'b dot respodsible. Argue it out with the policebad.

(*Enter Clara King.*)

CLARA: Good morning.

DICK: (*Rising.*) Good borning, Biss Kig.

MR. W.: (*Getting up.*) Women everywhere! Can't women do without their breakfast once in a while? (*Exit.*)

DICK: How are you Biss Kig?

CLARA: Oh very well. You must be tired after all that excitement way past your bedtime. Of course I'm used to it— I never go to bed until two in St. Joseph.

DICK: You dow, Biss Kig—bay I call you Biss Clara?—you bade a barked ibpressiod od me last dight.

CLARA: Did I?

DICK: Yes, id fact I cad remember—ah—that ady other girl ever bade that exact impressiod od be before.

(*Enter Hulda.*)

HULDA: Do you want coffee?

DICK: Yes. (*To Clara.*) Tell be, are you—?

HULDA: Weak or strong?

DICK: She is deither.

CLARA: She's speaking of coffee.

DICK: Strog. (*Exit Hulda.*) What was I sayig?

CLARA: How should I know?

DICK: I thought you bight have bed paying attedtion.

CLARA: Oh yes, it was something sentimental, I believe.

DICK: Listed, I remember, it's this—ever since I saw you I've been head over heels in love. Last dight my pulse began climbing up to one hudred and ten. I said to byself—"You're id love" and well—you know how it is. Between you ad by hay-fever I didn't sleep a wick—oh, Clara, for you I would give—

HULDA: (*Entering.*) Your coffee, sir.

DICK: Damn my coffee!

CLARA: Decidedly. Damn it with your napkin; it's running all over the table.

DICK: Here at your feet I cast my—

CLARA: Vanity.

DICK: Very well. If you persist in being facetious I can go you know. Goodbye.

CLARA: Oh, goodbye. Are you going to play cops and robbers with your little companions?

DICK: Cops and robbers! Bah! (*Exit.*)

(*Clara crosses to right hand wardrobe and opens door. Enter Josephus.*)

JO.: Well.

CLARA: Are you satisfied? You caused enough trouble last night.

JO.: Trouble—after you locked me in!

CLARA: Don't think you can fool me with those stories. You've got to get out of that costume.

JO.: The costumer didn't tell me it would run. I'm covered with deep crimson from head to foot.

CLARA: Serves you right. Now listen— I'll get you some clothes, I'll leave them on this chair. When I sneeze you come out and get them.

Jo.: Very well, but hurry up! (*He goes in closet. She exits.*)
(*Enter Cecile. The closet door opens, enter Will.*)

Will: Oh, Cecile!

Cec.: Oh Will! I'm sorry but I had to lock you in last night. How did you get out?

Will: I didn't know you locked me in.

Cec.: Why, yes.

Will: I must have broken the lock. I had to come out— I was suffocating. I had a terrible time. I'd just gotten out of one muddle when some woman held me up and insisted on searching me for ten thousand dollars. At last I convinced her I didn't have it and she went away—out the window—and I returned to the —ah—guest room.

Cec.: How odd. I wonder who it was? But I'm getting used to excitement. Nothing bothers me now.

Will: Well, what shall I do?

Cec.: Wait— I'll get you a coat. I'll leave it on this chair. When I open the window you come out and get it.

Will: Very well, when you open the window.
(*Exit both.*)
(*Enter Hulda. She hums a Swedish song, then opens window. Jo's door begins to open.*)

Hulda: Oh what a draft! (*She sneezes. Will's door begins to open. She goes out. Will and Josephus come slowly to center and then see each other.*)

Both: Well, what the devil!

Will: What are you doing here?

Jo.: What are you doing here?

Will: It's a long story.

Jo.: So's mine.

Will: Well, I know how you feel. Does your color run?

Jo.: Like a race horse. (*Aside.*) I wonder where those clothes are?

Will: Where can that coat be? Sh! there's someone coming.

Jo.: I'm not going back to that closet.

Will: Let's try the table.
(*They get under table. Hulda shows in Second Story Salle. Enter Mr. Wetherby.*)

Mr. W.: Who the deuce left this hat and coat in my room? It isn't mine.

S. S. S.: Pardon me, sir, but I 'ave a line of books h'I'd like to get you h'interested h'in.

Mr. W.: Books? I don't want books.

S. S. S.: I have "Innocent As A Flower" by Margureta Du Chene and "Delia the Double-died" by Madame Caruse. I also have a small encyclopedia and sets of Richard 'arding Davis and Rudyard Kipling. If ee take that ee get the Oswego Medical Review for six months or else you can have "Fireside Hours" for three months—

Mr. W.: Oh get out, get out! Haven't I got trouble enough. Hulda show her the door. (*Exit Mr. W.*)

S. S. S.: Well, there's the deuce to pay. I 'arvn't got the money. Some chap dressed up like the devil frighted me so I dropped it and later when I searched him he denied that 'e 'ad hit.

Hulda: Sh! I got the money, up in my room. I picked it up where you dropped it. Wait here and I'll get it for you. (*Exit.*)

S. S. S.: I carn't wait here. I'll step out into the 'allway. Blarst the bloomin' Swede. I 'ope she'll 'urry. (*Exit.*)

(*Enter Hulda with money.*)

Hulda: Salle, oh Salle! (*Snores.*) What's that? It's somebody coming. Where shall I put this money? I'll put it in here. (*Slips money into coat pocket. Exit.*)

(*Enter Cecile with clothes. She goes to window and opens it. No result. She tries again. Enter Clara with clothes, opposite door. She sees Cecile.*)

Cec.: Oh, good morning.

Clara: Good morning.

Cec.: What's that?

Clara: It's one of my guardian's suits; I'm taking it to the cleaners. What's that?

Cec.: Oh, this is one of father's suits; I'm taking it to the pressers.

Clara: Where I come from the cleaners and pressers are the same.

Cec.: How odd! It's different here. The—ah—cleaners clean and the—ah—pressers press. Ah! ha. Yes.

Clara: You surprise me.

Cec.: Can't I take your suit with mine?

Clara: Oh no, thank you.

(*They go to different sides of stage and eye each other. Cecile starts for window.*)

CEC.: Where are you going?

CLARA: It's hot in here. I'm going to open the window.

CEC.: Oh don't, don't! For heaven's sake don't open the window.

CLARA: Why not?

CEC.: Because I have a cold. (*Coughs.*) I'm going to sneeze. K—

CLARA: Don't sneeze, don't, don't. (*Puts hand over her mouth.*)

CEC.: Why not?

CLARA: The germs—the bubonic plague germs are spread like that.

CEC.: (*Indignantly.*) Do you mean to say I have the bubonic plague?

CLARA: No, but one must be careful. Well, I think I shall be going. Goodbye. (*Exit.*)

CEC.: Thank heavens! (*Goes to closet and opens it.*) Gone! gone! (*Exit hurriedly.*)

(*Enter Clara and Dickie.*)

CLARA: Oh heavens, can I never be alone!

DICK: Clara, Clara, I've been hunting for you for ten minutes.

CLARA: Leave me, please.

DICK: I shall never leave you until you say you'll bury me. Will you bury me?

CLARA: Yes, I'll bury you with the greatest of pleasure, but get out. (*Exit Dickie.*)

(*Looking in closet.*) Why he's gone. How odd! (*Exit.*)

(*Will comes out from under table.*)

WILL: He's asleep, thank the Lord. Oh, my own coat and hat at last. Now to get out of here. (*Exit.*)

JO.: (*Coming out from under table.*) I must have fallen asleep. I wonder where that other fellow is.

(*Enter Dickie.*)

DICK: Hello, who's this? Why it's a man! I say, you cad't be seen id those clothes—we've got to sell this house.

JO.: But I say, let me—

DICK: Not a word. Mr. Hendrix mustn't see you and I'b in a killing bood today.

JO.: But I am—

DICK: I don't care who you are. Here, lie down there until I return. Remember, if you make a sound you're dead.

JO.: Pardon me, if I make a sound I am alive.

DICK: Dead.

Jo.: Alive.

Dick: Dead—so lie down— I'll be back in a minute. (*Exit.*)

(*Enter Mr. W. and Mme. Zada.*)

Mr. W.: Good heavens, Amelia, haven't I got troubles enough?

Mme.: I dropped in to see how your guests were this morning.

Mr. W.: Guests— Lord, this morning they've taken to stealing things! There's ten thousand missing. I'd like to lay my hands on that ghost— I'd throttle him— I'd— Oh— Oh—

(*Josephus trembles under rug.*)

Mme.: Ten thousand dollars.

Mr. W.: Oh Lord, here's someone coming. You'll have to hide somewhere. Here, get under there. (*Puts her under table. Enter Dickie.*)

Dick: Ah good borning.

Mr. W.: I think I saw you before this morning.

Dick: Ah yes. —How'll I get him away? Ah, I have it. (*Produces pipe.*) I hope you don't mind my pipe.

Mr. W.: No, I rather like it. (*Makes grimace. Jo starts to rise. Dickie beats him back.*)

(*Enter Will and Policeman.*)

1st Pol.: I found this fellow standing on the front steps. What'll I do with him?

Will: Oh, how do you do, Mr. Wetherby? Hello, Dickie.

Dick: Ah, how delighted to see you I'm sure.

Mr. W.: Charmed.

Dick: Officer, this fellow is all right. —Keep down.—

Will: Why, what's the matter.

Dick: I was talking to my temper. I'm trying to keep my temper down. Keep down temper!

Will: Why have you got all the policemen around the house? That business last night?

Both: How did you hear about it?

Will: Why—er—her—ha—er, it was in the paper.

Both: Oh Lord!

(*Enter policeman with Second Story Salle. He is followed by Hulda, Miss Spigot, Clara and Cecile.*)

2d Pol.: I caught this woman trying to sneak out the back way. It looks a lot like the woman called Second Story Salle.

Mr. W.: It's the book agent!

Dick: You better hold her and search her.

2D POL.: She 'asn't got nothing suspicious on her but I'm taking no chances. She goes down to jail with me to be identified.

MR. W.: That's right, officer; do your duty.

S. S. S.: If you want to know who the guilty party is look there. (*Points to Will.*) Search him.

(*They search Will and find bank notes.*)

DICK: The ten thousand, thank heavens!

MISS S.: My nephew!

HULDA: I told you he'd land in penitentiary, like Ole.

WILL: Officer, this is ridiculous. I never saw this overcoat until five minutes ago—that is since last night.

S. S. S.: Don't ye believe him.

WILL: Why, Mr. Wetherby can testify to my character.

MR. W.: I'm doing no testifying.

2D POL.: I guess you both better go down with me.

S. S. S.: The deuce you say! (*Produces pistol.*) Don't move or I'll put a bullet through you. I'll need plenty of time so I guess you had all better sit down on the floor. Now where is that ten thousand dollars? Turn out your pockets! Ah, but my taxi bill is amounting up outside so I'll not have time to search— Ta ta! (*Exit Second Story Salle in haste.*) Ta-ta— (*She goes out, policeman after her.*) (*They start after her and discover Jo.*)

ALL: Who's this— It's another one—(*etc.*)

MR. W.: It must be the pal she spoke of.

JO.: Pardon me—

CEC.: Another devil!

JO.: No, I am—

CLARA: It's guardian!

DICK: (*Tears off mustache.*)

MR. W.: Cousin Josephus!

ALL: Mr. Hendrix!

POLICEMAN: Shall I arrest him?

MR. W.: What are you doing in that costume?

JO.: I'm—I'm— —

MR. W.: I see your plot. So it was you all the time?

ALL: For shame!

JO.: I'll not be insulted— I'll leave the house. Give me my money and I'll go.

POLICEMAN: Why it's gone!

DICK: Hasn't anybody got it?

ALL: It was on the table. No!

JO: Find me my money quick, all of you. I'll sue the police department. Oh Lord! (*Sinks into chair. All go out. Mme. Z. crawls out from under the table.*)

MME.: Josephus! My Josephus!

JO.: A voice from the dead! Amelia, what are you doing here?

MME.: My husband, oh my husband!

JO.: What do you want?

MME.: You, I want you!

JO.: You can't have me.

MME.: You loved me once!

JO.: Five years ago. When I married you I was a clerk and you a manicure girl. When I rose in life I had to leave you. Your station was too humble.

MME.: Is there not a touch of sentiment left in you? Have you forgotten the moonlight nights when we set on the terrace and I (*sob*) polished your finger nails?

JO.: Don't weep on me; you'll get me damp and I take cold easily.

MME.: Yes I remember when you proposed to me you had a cold. Oh, Josephus, won't you take me back?

JO.: Oh I suppose I'll have to.

MME.: Well, in that case here's your ten thousand dollars.

JO.: Where did you get it?

MME.: I purloined it in the excitement. Come, we'll face the world together. (*Exit.*)

(*Enter Mr. W. and Will.*)

WILL: Mr. W., as contracting engineer for the Red Wing, Hastings and Minneapolis Railroad I am authorized to offer you fifteen thousand dollars for your house.

MR. W.: Fifteen thousand? Thank heavens, that saves us! Yes, I'll take it. Yes and thank you, Will, you're not as bad as the rest of them.

(*Enter Cecile.*)

CEC.: Oh Father, I've been looking for you. Cousin Josephus says he has got his money. He's walking off with a strange woman.

MR. W.: Thank the Lord! Thank the Lord! (*Exit.*)

CEC.: Oh I'm so tired I feel as if I could sleep for weeks.

WILL: So am I. That night in that little hole. After this I'm going to be careful what I wear. Oh, Cecile!

CEC.: Yes.

WILL: Sleepy?
CEC.: Yes, are you?
WILL: Yes, but before I go to sleep I want to ask you something—will you marry me?
CEC.: Yes, I suppose so. Do you love me?
WILL: Yes, I always have.
CEC.: So've I.
CEC.: —st—st—!
WILL: —st—st—! } (*They are both asleep.*)

(*Curtain.*)

Textual Apparatus

Textual Introduction

I

THE TEXTUAL apparatus consists of as many as four sections, where appropriate, for each work, (1) "Textual Commentary," (2) "Textual Notes," (3) "Editorial Emendations in the Copy-Text," and (4) "End-of-Line Hyphenation in the Copy-Text."

Textual Commentary identifies the copy-text for each work and comments upon unusual features in the text which require extended discussion.

Textual Notes discusses those emendations and refusals to emend which require explanation, and includes as well other brief discussions of certain characteristics of the copy-text.

Editorial Emendations lists all emendations made for the present edition with the exception of regularizations specified in the "Textual Introduction." The emended reading is to the left of the bracket. The rejected copy-text reading is to the right; "*omitted*" means that the reading does not appear in the copy-text. A wavy line (~) stands for the word cited to the left of the bracket and indicates that only a punctuation mark has been emended. A caret (‸) calls attention to the absence of a punctuation mark. An asterisk beside an emendation indicates that the reading is discussed in a textual note. The notation "*stet*" indicates a refusal to emend where an emendation might conceivably have been made. Wherever copy-text is a Fitzgerald holograph manuscript, the notation "M" (followed by a semicolon) indicates that the emended reading agrees with the transcription reading. The notation "M" does not take into account regularizations of stage directions and speech headings noted in the "Textual Introduction."

End-of-Line Hyphenation is a list of editorially established forms of possible compounds which were hyphenated at the ends of lines in the copy-text.

In determining line references, every line, with the exception of running heads and rules, is to be counted separately. This is also true for pages with bracketed material. Thus, for example, two names bracketed with one line of dialogue between them count as three lines.

II

All of the manuscripts and the typescript used in preparing this edition are in Princeton University Library. *The Girl from Lazy J*, Fitzgerald's earliest St. Paul play, exists in two versions, an extremely rough draft in Fitzgerald's hand, almost complete, but with many errors in spelling and punctuation, and a transcription in the hand of Elizabeth Magoffin, complete but with many emendations of Fitzgerald's manuscript. *The Captured Shadow*, Fitzgerald's second play, also exists in two versions, one in Fitzgerald's hand, again with many errors and this time with the conclusion missing, and, once again, a transcription in Elizabeth Magoffin's hand, complete but with many emendations of Fitzgerald's manuscript. Only a few pages of *Coward*, the third St. Paul play, are extant in Fitzgerald's hand, but a complete version is available in Elizabeth Magoffin's hand. A comparison of Fitzgerald's holograph with the equivalent sections in the transcription once again shows many variants. *Assorted Spirits*, the fourth St. Paul play, is available complete in typescript with changes in ink in two different hands, one of which is Elizabeth Magoffin's. The identity of the typist or typists is unknown.

Fitzgerald's holographs have been used as copy-text in this edition when available, and, for the most part, the author's substantives have been rendered unchanged. (Since Fitzgerald's dialogue and stage directions almost always clearly suggest the action, only a few necessary stage directions have been added—mainly from the transcriptions—and these are all noted in the list of emendations.) On the other hand, because the errors and omissions in punctuation and errors in spelling are so numerous and because of the hardship to the reader that would result if Fitzgerald's text were reproduced without correction, I have emended accidentals extensively but conservatively. Except as listed in section III of this introduction, no attempt has been made to regularize spelling or punctuation. I take responsibility for all emendations but record for historical interest with the letter "M" those cases in which my changes agree with Elizabeth Magoffin's.

Wherever a Fitzgerald holograph is not available, a transcription has been used as copy-text. In this case, emendations have been kept to a minimum and have been employed mainly to correct outright errors or situations possibly causing reader confusion. Thus, for example, typographical errors such as "Lst" instead of "1st," confusing demonstrable errors such as "bable" instead of "babble," the non-authorial and misleading "'ld" ending for contractions in Elizabeth Magoffin's transcriptions, and uncancelled but contradictory material at points of insert have been corrected.

The reader is referred to the "Textual Commentary" for each play for a more detailed discussion of individual copy-text problems.

III

The following details are rendered uniform in all of the plays: (1) in the list of characters, etc., preceding each play, settings and identification of characters have been italicized; (2) stage directions incorrectly placed immediately following speeches have been placed separately immediately below; (3) stage directions have been italicized and placed in parentheses, the first word is always capitalized, and a terminal period is always placed before the final parenthesis; (4) speech headings have been set in full caps and are always followed by a colon; (5) names of characters in speech headings have been regularized; for example, in *Coward*, "Cecilia" (Fitzgerald's spelling in his holograph) is used instead of his shortened form "Celia," his abbreviations "Cec." or "Cec," and Elizabeth Magoffin's "Cecelia" and "Celia"; however, in the speeches, the variant form "Celia" has been retained; (6) redundant speech headings have been deleted.

Where Fitzgerald's holograph is used as copy-text, regularity has been imposed on the following without notation in the table of emendations: (1) periods omitted at the end of sentences have been added; however, where both terminal punctuation and the following capitalization are omitted, the emendation is listed; (2) periods omitted after abbreviations have been added; (3) periods placed erroneously in the middle of sentences have been deleted; (4) commas before capitalized words beginning new sentences are emended to periods; (5) apparent dashes at the end of complete sentences are emended to periods since in the case of Fitzgerald's handwriting it is impossible to distinguish the two; (6) all proper names and titles incorrectly lower cased are capitalized; (7) lower-cased words following terminal punctuation are capitalized; (8) all family appellations such as "Father," "Mother," etc., used as names are regarded as proper nouns and capitalized; (9) apostrophes erroneously omitted from contractions—or other words, such as " 'em" (i.e., "them"), requiring apostrophes to indicate omitted letters—have been added; (10) all misplaced apostrophes have been placed correctly; (11) quotation marks indicating the beginning and end of speeches have been deleted; (12) inconsistent placement of punctuation marks coupled with quotation marks has been corrected; (13) quotations within quotations are made to follow the usual "'. . .'" pattern; (14) numbers and sums of money have generally been spelled out; (15) superscript letters and figures have been lowered; (16) ampersands have been expanded to "and."

The following details are regularized where the transcriptions are used as copy-text: (1) periods erroneously omitted at the end of sentences have been added; Elizabeth Magoffin habitually left them out of sentences followed by stage directions; (2) periods omitted after abbreviations have been supplied; (3) capitalization of words after semicolons—a consistent practice of Elizabeth Magoffin—has been removed; (4) all family appellations such as "Father," "Mother," etc., used as names are regarded as proper names and capitalized; (5) inconsistent placement of punctuation marks coupled with quotation marks has been corrected; (6) quotations within quotations are made to follow the usual "' . . . '" pattern; (7) variant spacing in contractions has been regularized; (8) misplaced or omitted apostrophes in contractions have been corrected; (9) superscript letters and figures have been lowered; (10) numbers and sums of money have generally been spelled out; (11) all dashes (and single hyphens used as dashes in the typescript) indicating sudden breaks in thought, interruptions in speech, or those used as final punctuation have been replaced by em dashes— and when dashes have been used as final punctuation, the spacing following has been regularized to conform to normal terminal spacing; (12) ampersands have been expanded to "and"; (13) single parenthesis marks typed above each other as substitutes for braces have been replaced with braces; (14) directions and symbols for insertion have been deleted as have the various red, blue, yellow, etc., markings denoting entrances, exits, and other similar directions; (15) in *Assorted Spirits*, because Fitzgerald's preference is unknown, the spelling "Dickie" has been adopted throughout instead of the transcription's inconsistent "Dickie," "Dicky," and "Dickey."

The Girl from Lazy J

Textual Commentary

The Girl from Lazy J exists in two versions, Fitzgerald's holograph and a transcription in the hand of Elizabeth Magoffin. Fitzgerald's holograph, in pencil, is in all likelihood his last draft despite its many cancellations and revisions. It consists of six leaves, partially unpaginated, white wove paper with blue rules, measuring 26.2 x 19.9 cm., and a seventh, trimmed from the bottom section of a leaf of similar paper, measuring approximately 3.2 x 19.9 cm. A perforation at the top left of the six leaves indicates that they were attached at one time. At the top of page 1 is the title 'The girl from Lazy J—' trebly underlined. This first page (its verso blank) contains a revision of the cancelled title and cast found on the unnumbered verso of page 2 as well as Fitzgerald's original beginning of the play with Jack (rather than Langford, or Lang, the hero's name in much of the remainder of the holograph) Darcy calling for Tony Gonzoles, his cowhand. Later, Fitzgerald added—on the recto of the sixth unnumbered leaf—Jack's preceding statements reflecting his elation over his engagement to Leticia Larned and his concern about his mother's reaction. A small amount of dialogue to be inserted before Tony's first exit is also on the recto of the sixth leaf. The action resumes at the middle of page 2 (the upper part of the page contains a cancelled early version of some of the dialogue found on page 1) with a notation at the end of the sixth line directing the reading to yet another insert found on the recto of the sixth leaf. At the bottom of page 2, Fitzgerald introduced the theme of the mysterious note from "D. S. H." and continued this onto page 3 with the discussion between Lang and his uncle about the former remaining awake to guard the house from the unknown villain. In the middle of this page a notation directs the reader to page 4 (which Fitzgerald originally numbered as 3), Lang's conversation with his aunt about his engagement. (The beginning of this conversation is to be found on the 3.2 x 19.9 cm. trimmed section—also numbered 3, its verso containing some cancelled material—that was at one time pinned to the blank verso of page 3.) The action resumes on page 5 (which Fitzgerald originally numbered as 4)—where Lang's aunt exits and the evil Tony sneaks in and ties up Lang—and then at the bottom of page 3 where Leticia enters and confronts Tony. The fifth leaf, recto and verso unpaginated, contains the conclusion of the play (an asterisk on the recto—immediately after Mr. Kendall apprehends Leticia—requires the insertion of two brief speeches found on the verso of leaf 6), and the final sixth leaf, also unpaginated recto and verso, contains, in addition to the inserts mentioned, Fitzgerald's summary plan for his conclusion.

Elizabeth Magoffin's transcription consists of four sheets of white wove paper with blue rules measuring 39.2 x 31.7 cm. folded folio to form eight leaves, all unnumbered, each measuring approximately 31.7 x 19.6 cm. and attached on the left with three brass fasteners. Pasted on the recto of the first leaf is an approximately 21 x 17.3 cm. rough drawing of the cast in black ink on white paper with blue rules, possibly the work of Dorothy Greene, a member of the cast. The transcription, all in blue ink except for a few words in black ink, is in Elizabeth Magoffin's hand. At the top of the recto of the first leaf appears ' "◇O" ', and below is the title 'The Girl from "Lazy J" | by | Francis Scott Fitzgerald | (An Original Sketch)'; the verso of this leaf is blank. The play is written on both sides of the following five leaves and the recto of the sixth. The remainder is blank.

In the absence of any proof that another version in Fitzgerald's hand ever existed or that the not quite fifteen-year-old author dictated the transcription, one must surmise that Elizabeth Magoffin was responsible for most if not all of the differences between Fitzgerald's holograph and the transcription. Fitzgerald apparently relied heavily on Miss Magoffin to copy the sections in correct order, add or correct speech headings, and especially to correct the young Fitzgerald's extremely erratic spelling and punctuation. But, in addition, while making this transcription, Elizabeth Magoffin made more than one hundred substantive changes in what Fitzgerald had originally written. A very few of these, such as "it's a dreary night" and "he's always" instead of Fitzgerald's "it a dreary night" and "he's alway," were necessary corrections of obvious errors. And, of course, correcting the hero's name from "Lang" and "Langford" to "Jack" was also a necessity as were at least a few of the added stage directions. But many of the remaining substantive changes cannot be as easily justified or explained. Once in a while, for example, Fitzgerald's colloquial language was changed to more formal English with, however, a lack of consistency. "Be sure and put" was changed to "be sure to put," but "sit up and await developments" was retained. Some of Fitzgerald's contracted forms, such as "Uncle's," "there's," and "you're," were written out; on the other hand, contractions such as "Tony's" and "they're" were left unchanged. Of course, despite the lack of rationale here, one could argue that Fitzgerald's participation in the production was tantamount to approval of the transcription. But it seems just as likely that in relinquishing the chore of copying his manuscript, Fitzgerald obligingly acceded to Elizabeth Magoffin's amateurish editing which changed the author's final draft. Since there is no evidence that Fitzgerald was responsible for these changes, the holograph is used as copy-text here.

Further, there is no proof that Fitzgerald was responsible for the first of two minor variations in plot between the holograph and the transcription. This first variation begins at the point where the nefarious Tony Gonzoles ties up Jack. In the holograph, Tony immediately tries to open the cabinet containing Mr. Kendall's money, but Leticia Larned intercedes. Later, when Tony attempts to escape, Jack shoots him. In the transcription, however, Tony considers shooting Jack before searching for the money. "Now I will have my revenge," he sneers. But then he changes his mind about using the gun, reaches for his knife, hesitates again, exclaims, "But wait," and goes to the cabinet. When Leticia disarms him, she places this knife on a nearby table. Thus, according to the transcription, when Tony makes his escape attempt, he grabs this knife and then loses it during a struggle with Jack who then stabs and kills the blackmailer.

Since the holograph version of this episode is complete, and since Fitzgerald's plot summary on leaf 6 echoes the holograph version, I have not emended in this case.

On the other hand, Fitzgerald's summary suggests at least the possibility of approval, if not authorship, of the second variation in plot; only in the transcription does Jack—at the end of the play—receive a telegram from his mother acknowledging his engagement to Leticia. In his summary Fitzgerald wrote, "Leticia unmasks. Debris cleared way. 'Bless you children.'"

The middle phrase suggests that he wanted all aspects of the plot, at this point, resolved satisfactorily. As a result, the emendation from the transcription has been adapted into this edition.

Textual Notes

16.28-33 Kendall . . . developments.] 'You . . . exactly' (16.31-32) was added later without speech headings and with vertical lines directing the reader ambiguously to points of insertion. Magoffin transcribed this as 'Kendell— (Looks again at note) But look, it says "on the night of the 12th," and this is the twelfth! You don't think he'll really come, do you?' 'Jack— Not exactly (Looks again at note) So it does. Do you want me to sit up and await developments?' Despite the transcription's many emendations at this point, Magoffin's reading—with Jack's vague reference 'So it does'—is still awkward.

18.5 *masked.*] Fitzgerald's error. The reader has to know why Jack does not recognize Leticia. Magoffin's reading here is 'Letitia appears, masked.'

18.6 *work*] I.e., pry open; retained despite possible ambiguity

18.13 you.] In holograph, followed by 'You' and illegible word. Magoffin's reading used here.

18.25 (*Noticing Jack. Aside.*)] Added here to avoid possible confusion. Leticia has been talking to Kendall, and suddenly, for the first time, realizes that Jack has been present.

18.27 *Mr. Kendall*] In the holograph, Fitzgerald omitted Kendall's name because 'unties Gonzoles' originally followed 'gun.' (18.23). Fitzgerald then inserted an asterisk and a caret indicating insertion of the intervening material which appears elsewhere in the holograph.

18.35-19.2 (*Enter . . . Leticia.*)] From Magoffin's transcription; see "Textual Commentary." Fitzgerald's spelling of 'Leticia' and 'Kendall' used here instead of Magoffin's 'Letitia' and 'Kendell'.

19.7-16 *Description* . . . letters.] Furnishings and properties list from Magoffin's transcription. Fitzgerald's spelling of 'Leticia' and 'Kendall' again used here.

Editorial Emendations in the Copy-Text

15.1 *The . . . J*‸] The girl from Lazy J— *triple underlining*

15.3 *Ranch*] M; ranch *also emended at 15.8*
15.5 *11:45*] M; 11.45
15.5 *12:15*] M; 12.15
15.7 KENDALL,] M; ~^
15.10 DARCY,] M; ~^
15.12 *cowpuncher*] M; cow puncher
15.13 *rises,*] ~^
15.13 *chair,*] M; ~^
15.13 *whistling*] whisleling
15.14 JACK:] M; *omitted; also emended at 16.1; 16.32; 17.8; 17.14; 17.16; 17.18; 17.20; 17.22; 17.25; 18.29*
15.14 accepted,] Accepted^
15.14 jingo,] M; Jingo^
15.15 Mississippi] M; Missisipi
15.15 her.] ~^
15.15 She's] M; she's
15.16 say. And] ~^ and
15.16 say,] ~^
15.17 care?] M; ~.
15.19 Why,] M; ~^
15.20 My,] M; ~^
15.21 no,] ~^
15.21-22 (*Noise . . . Rises.*)] M; *omitted*
15.22 that?] M; ~^
15.23 Tony!] M; ~,
15.25 *Kendall,*] M; ~^
15.25 *Tony*] M; Jim
15.25 *before*] M; befor
15.26 KENDALL:] M; *omitted; also emended at 16.3; 16.16; 18.21*
15.26 horses,] M; ~^
15.27 scoundrel?] ~.
15.27 you,] ~^
15.27 Tony,] Jim^
15.28 you?] M; ~.
15.29 git,] M; ~^
15.29 before] M; befor
15.30 (*To Jack.*)] M; *omitted*
15.31 anything?] M; ~^
16.1 (*To Tony.*)] M; *omitted*

16.1 José] M; Jose
16.1 now. It's] ~^ its
16.2 *Tony*] M; *omitted*
16.3 think,] M; ~^
16.7 careful] M; carful
16.7 Mexicans,] ~^
16.7 Uncle. They'd] ~^ they'd
16.8 Tony's] M; Jims
16.9 Huh!] M; ~^
16.9 They're] M; There
16.9 horses. They] ~^ they
16.10 haven't] havn't
16.14 JACK^:] M; L.—*also emended at 16.27; 16.30; 17.3*
16.14 way,] M; ~^
16.16 scamp!] M; ~^
16.16 What] what
16.17 J?] ~.
16.17 Leticia,] M; ~^
16.17 hey?] Hey.
16.17 say,] M; ~^
16.18 received] M; received *also emended at 16.22*
16.20 JACK:] M; L—*also emended at 16.35*
16.22 steers] M; stears
16.23 sincerely—^] sincerly . .
16.23 things!] M; ~,
16.25 Well,] M; ~^
16.25 it?] M; ~.
16.26 go?] M; go^
16.27 it?] M; ~.
*16.28-33 KENDALL . . . developments.] *stet*
16.28 the twelfth] M; twelfth
16.31 KENDALL:] *omitted*
16.31 really] M; realy
16.31 come?] ~^
16.38 Yes,] M; ~^
17.1 way,] M; ~^
17.1 anything] M; any thing
17.4 night. And] M; ~^ and
17.4 sleepy,] M; ~^

17.6 *Jack*] Lang *also emended at 18.5*
17.7 MRS. KENDALL:] M; *omitted; also emended at 17.9; 17.13; 17.15; 17.17; 17.19; 17.21; 17.23; 17.26*
17.7 bed,] M; ~^
17.7 Jack?] M; Lang.
17.8 while,] M; ~^
17.9 Hello!] M; ~^
17.9 Someone] Somone
17.10 catch.] ~^
17.10 It] M; it
17.12 JACK:] M; Lang—*also emended at 17.31*
17.12 Auntie,] M; Auntie^
17.12 something] M; somthing
17.13 it?] ~^
17.15 You're] Your
17.15 engaged?] M; ~.
17.15 Jack,] M; ~^
17.15 you're] M; your
17.16 No,] M; ~^
17.17 say?] M; ~.
17.18 her,] M; ~^
17.19 me,] M; ~^
17.19 to?] M; ~.
17.21 Larned?] M; ~.
17.23 Jack,] M; Langford^
17.23 you'll] you'l
17.25 and,] ~^
17.25 Auntie,] M; ~^
17.26 some time,] M; sometime^
17.27 I suppose] M; suppose
17.27 a] M; *omitted (torn away)*
17.28 girl] M; g
17.28 Well,] M; ~^
17.29 night. Come] M; ~^ come
17.29 you're] your
17.33 My, it's] M; My^ it
17.33 Hello!] M; ~,
17.34 something] somthing
17.35 Tony's] Jim's

17.36 First,] M; 1st^
17.37 horses.] M; ~^
17.38 And he's] and he's
17.38 always] M; alway
17.39 "D. S. H."] M; ^D^ S^ H.^
18.2 *Tony*] M; J
18.2 *around*,] ~^
18.3 *candle*] candal
18.3 *Jack*] M; Lang
18.3-4 *himself*] M; him self
18.4 *Leticia*] M; Let.
*18.5 *masked.*] M; *omitted*
18.5 *She*] she
*18.6 *work*] M; *stet*
18.6-7 *cabinet. She*] cabinet^ she
18.7 *hides*] M; hide
18.8 LETICIA:] M; *omitted; also emended at 18.13; 19.4*
18.10 Now] M; ow *(partially torn away)*
18.10 Gonzoles,] M; ~^
18.10 Hoskins,] ~^
18.10 are] M; *omitted; (torn away)*
18.11 night?] M; ~.
18.12 TONY:] M; *omitted*
18.13 Hush! Not] M; ~^ not
*18.13 you.] M; you. You
18.15 ago?] ~.
18.16 or,] ~^
18.16 live,] M; ~^
18.16 three.] ~,
18.18 purpose,] M; ~^
18.19 *door^ with*] ~. With
18.21 holy,] ~^
18.21 woman!] M; ~^
18.21 D.S.H.,] ~. ~. ~^^
18.22 whatever] M; what ever
18.22 are,] ~^
18.23 eh?] ~.
*18.25 (*Noticing Jack. Aside.*)] *omitted*
18.26 presence] presents

18.26 here?] ~‸
*18.27 *Mr. Kendall*] *omitted*
18.27 *Gonzoles*,] ~‸
18.29 you're] M; your
18.29 blackmailer] M; black mailer
18.29 Yes,] M; ~‸
18.30 that!] M; ~.
18.30 Uncle,] M; ~‸
18.31 girl is,] M; ~ ~‸
18.31 whoever] M; who ever
18.31 she is,] M; ~ ~‸
18.32 tonight,] ~.
18.32 Tony,] M; ~‸
18.32 Hoskins,] ~‸
18.33 stabbed me] M; stabed
18.33 before] M; befor
18.33 getaway] get away
18.33 (*Walks toward Leticia.*)] M; *omitted*
18.34 whoever] M; who ever
18.34 are,] M; ~‸
18.34 you're] your
*18.35-19.2 (*Enter . . . Leticia.*)] M; *omitted*
19.1 girl,] ~‸
19.3 Leticia!] M; ~'
19.4 Jack!] M; ~‸
19.5 you,] M; ~‸
19.6 (*Curtain.*)] M; *omitted*
*19.7-16 *Description* . . . letters.] M; *omitted*
19.7 rancher's] Rancher's
19.13 Leticia] Letitia
19.14 Kendall] Kendell *also emended at 19.15*
19.16 Shotgun] Shot gun

The Captured Shadow

TEXTUAL COMMENTARY

Two versions of *The Captured Shadow* are extant. The first is Fitzgerald's holograph of 62 leaves (all versos are blank) in black ink with many corrections and markings in blue and black ink, red and purple crayon, and pencil. Fitzgerald's signature appears as part of the cast listing, leaf 2, and in pencil in the left margin of leaf 54. A few punctuation marks and possibly a word or two may be in the hand of Elizabeth Magoffin. The leaves, white wove paper with blue rules, many with torn edges, measure approximately 26.2 x 20 cm., have perforations at the top indicating that they were fastened together at one time, and are foliated 2, 4-64 in pencil. The missing leaves presumably included the title and other information as well as the ending of the play coinciding with the bottom of leaf 50 and all of leaf 51 of the second version of *The Captured Shadow* at Princeton University Library.

This second version, a transcription of Fitzgerald's holograph in Elizabeth Magoffin's hand, consists of 57 leaves foliated [*3*], 1-51, [52-54]; all versos are blank; the final leaf is blank on both sides; and all are held together at the top with two brass fasteners. Except for a few phrases in pencil and many markings for entrances and exits in blue crayon, all is in black ink. The paper, white wove with blue rules and 'CROWN BOND' watermark, measures approximately 25.2 x 20.1 cm. The title 'The | Captured | Shadow' (double underlined) in blue crayon appears alone in large handwriting on the recto of the first leaf.

Both texts are flawed. The title page and the very end of Fitzgerald's play are missing, and the cast list, an early tentative one, is torn and partly missing. Though Fitzgerald's holograph is not as rough a draft as that of his previous play, there are still errors in spelling and punctuation. But, on the other hand, the Magoffin transcription once again contains many changes, this time including some four hundred and fifty substantive emendations. Among them are the correction of informal language such as "anyways" to "anyway," "simply enough" to "simple enough," and "you're" to "you are"; the correction of syntax such as "a rather doubtful compliment" to "rather a doubtful compliment"; and the correction of attempts at dialect such as "kin" to "can" and seemingly purposeful slurring such as "wisout" to "without." Again, as in *The Girl from Lazy J*, it is difficult to find a consistency in the method of correcting, and it is not possible to explain all of the changes. In any event, here, too, it seems improbable that the young author dictated these changes. Thus, where it exists, Fitzgerald's holograph has been used as copy-text, the title page and conclusion of the Magoffin transcription substituting for the holograph's missing title page and ending as well as Miss Magoffin's cast list replacing Fitzgerald's early tentative, torn list. A facsimile of Magoffin's "Plan of business," leaf [52] of the transcription, is included in this edition.

Textual Notes

25.1-34 *The* . . . Dorr] Magoffin's title page and cast (that of the production) used here rather than Fitzgerald's tentative cast list. 'Thorton,' 'Chinyman,' and 'McGinness'—consistent spellings in Fitzgerald's holograph—have been used, however, rather than Magoffin's consistent 'Thornton,' 'Chinaman,' and 'McGinnis.'

26.33 adrinkin'] Final 'g' in copy-text probably erroneous; Emma Kate drops her final 'g's' throughout the remainder of the scene.

30.16 wisout] Spelling retained as apparently a purposeful attempt to reflect Hubert's slurred inebriated speech rather than being another example of Fitzgerald's many misspellings.

30.33 edication] Spelling retained as possible purposeful illiteracy.

32.29 night,] Fitzgerald probably forgot to delete following 'and then' (deleted here) when he added 'we oughhnt to' (emended here to 'we oughtn't to'); Magoffin's reading used here.

37.18 *door.*)] In Fitzgerald's holograph, 'door and' followed by two illegible words. Magoffin's reading used here.

38.10-11 gen d'armes] Here and elsewhere Fitzgerald's French, despite the errors, is retained, especially since in the case of Dureal it may be an attempt to make the detective seem comic.

41.22 *from case on wall*] Fitzgerald originally wrote 'out of drawer,' then pencilled in 'wall' above 'drawer.' The phrase 'out of wall' makes little sense here; Magoffin's reading, probably reflecting Fitzgerald's intention, is used.

44.8 Shadow.] Followed by three illegible words not in Magoffin transcription.

50.33 *McGinness*] the Shadow has handed the key to someone; I have followed Magoffin's reading.

52.15 I] Fitzgerald's holograph ends here.

Editorial Emendations in the Copy-Text

25.1	^*The*] "The
25.1	*Shadow*^] Shadow"
25.3	Melodramatic] melodramatic
25.3	Comedy] comedy
25.10	presentation] presentaion
25.17	THORTON] Thornton
25.17	DUDLEY] Dudly
25.18	*Shadow*"] Shadow^
25.19	SAUNDERS] Saunder
25.19	*housekeeper*] houskeeper
25.30	CHINYMAN] Chinaman
25.31	McGINNESS] McGinnis
25.34	Dorr^] ~.
26.1	ACT I] M; *omitted*
26.2	*armchair*] arm chair
26.4	*Threads*] M; threads
26.4	*Among*] M; among
26.4	*Gold.*"] M; gold^^
26.12	mum] mumm *also emended at 26.14; 26.16; 26.21; 28.9*
26.13	doing?] M; ~.
26.14	Asleepin',] ~^
26.15	Sleeping,] M; ~^
26.17	o'clock?] M; oclock^
26.20	nothin',] M; nothin'^
26.21	it'ud] it ^ud
26.21	bit,] M; ~^
26.22	*Shrugging*] M; Shurging
26.22	out,] M; ~^
26.23	he?] M; ~.

26.24 Yes'm,] M; Yes'm^
26.25 way, please] M; ~. Please
26.31 him] M: *omitted*
26.31 piece] M; peice
26.33 mum,] mumm^ *also emended at 27.3; 27.10*
*26.33 adrinkin'] M; a drinking
26.34 every night] M; everynight
26.34 awalkin'] M; a walkin'
26.35 Connage's] M; Connages
27.1 eavesdropping,] M; ~^
27.1 you?] M; ~.
27.2 trick,] ~^
27.3 goodness,] M; ~^
27.3 hear] M; here
27.5 trick,] M; ~^
27.5 Kate,] M; ~^
27.7 say?] M; ~.
27.15 creatures, heigh-ho] ~^ Heigh-oh
27.17 I,] M; ~^
27.17 miss—] ~^
27.18 you,] M; ~^
27.19 tell?] M; ~.
27.20 ridiculous] M; rediculous
27.24 atellin'] M; a tellin'
27.27 us!] M; ~.
27.29 else?] M; ~.
27.30 some,] M; ~^
27.31 great!] M; Great^
27.33 without] M; with out
27.34 me! And] M; ~^ and
27.34 say?] M; ~^
28.1 ^Miss] '~
28.1 Saunders!^] M; ~)'
28.2 here,] M; ~^
28.3 *doorway*] door way
28.3 Saunders,] M; ~^
28.4 fascinating] M; facinating
28.5 Why,] M; ~^
28.5 here?] M; ~.
28.7 *Sniff*, *etc*.] ~^ ect^

28.8 tired?] M; ~∧
28.9 Tired? No] M; ~∧ no
28.10 chair,] M; ~∧
28.15 Saunders,] M; ~.
28.15 what's] Whats
28.15 sorehead?] ~∧
28.19-20 newspapers?] M; ~.
28.21 yes,] M; ~∧
28.24 Horrors!] M; ~∧
28.26 kind?] M; ~.
28.28 catch him] M; catch
28.31 Oh!] M; ~∧
28.32 accomplished!] M; ~∧
28.33 Oh! !] M; ~∧∧
28.34 wicked!] M; ~∧
28.35 Oh! ! !] M; ~∧∧∧
28.38 compliments] M; complements *also emended at 29.5; 29.6; 35.2*
28.39 does?] M; ~∧
29.1 that,] M; ~∧
29.1 they?] M; ~.
29.2 Unfortunately] M; Unfortuneatly
29.4 Really?] M ~∧
29.5 off] M; of
29.8 Yes,] M; ~∧
29.8-9 subject,] M; ~∧
29.10 brother?] M; ~∧
29.11 Saunders!] M; ~∧
29.15 Hubert, indeed!] ~∧ ~∧
29.16 *Girl's*] M; Girls
29.16 *outside*—] M; out side)
29.16 *singing*] M; *omitted*
29.16 *Everybody's*] M; Every bodies
29.16 *doin'*] doing
29.18 *doorway*] door way
29.19 about?] M; ~.
29.23 Mayburn,] M; ~∧
29.26 dear,] M; ~∧
29.27 Indeed!] M; ~.
29.30 Of] M; Oh

29.31 remember,] ~∧
29.32 you] M; *omitted*
29.34 Oh,] M; ~∧
29.39 Well,] M; ~∧
29.40 evening,] M; ~∧
30.4 chat,] M; ~∧
30.5 Hubert?] M; ~.
30.6 somewhere,] M; somwhere∧
30.14 Ah,] M; ~∧
30.14 now?] M; ~.
30.15-16 residence] M; residense
*30.16 wisout] *stet*
30.16 key,] ~∧
30.16 'specially] M; 'specialty
30.17 key?] M; ~.
30.17 aggravating] agravating
30.18 *outside*] M; out side
30.18 trick. Leave] ~∧ leave
30.19 me] M; my
30.19 up,] M; ~∧
30.24 in,] ~∧
30.25 *Rudd*,] M; ~∧
30.27 me,] M; ~∧
30.27 assistance?] M; assistence∧
30.30 Say,] M; ~∧
30.30 out?] M; ~∧
30.32 hemorrhage?] M; hemorage.
*30.33 edication] *stet*
30.34 Say,] ~∧
30.36 Mrs. Connage] M; Mrs. Connge
30.37 family,] M; ~∧
30.37 see,] M; ~∧
30.38 me,] M; ~∧
30.39 Dad,] dad∧
31.1(2x) one—] ~∧
31.1 me,] M; ~∧
31.1 No,] M; ~∧
31.2 four] M; for
31.3 for?] M; for.
31.4 Forty-seventh Street] M; forty∧~ street

31.7 Say,] ~∧
31.8 night,] ~∧
31.9 governor] M; guvoner
31.9 say?] M; ~.
31.10 "how-de-do."] ∧~∧~∧~.∧
31.13 No,] M; ~∧
31.13 cat,] M; ~∧
31.14 Divine,] M; ~∧
31.14 it,] M; ~∧
31.14 Ching?] M; ~.
31.15 Unsophisticating] M; Unsophistocating
31.17 Say,] M; ~∧
31.17 Charley's] M; Charelys
31.18 things] M; thing
31.19 *de*] M; De
31.19 swimmin'?] M; ~'∧
31.20 Mother?] M; ~.
31.21 bust?] M; ~.
31.27 lately] M; latly
31.28 curves] M; curve's
31.29 of] M; or
31.29 crooks] M; crook's
31.30 married?] M; ~∧
31.31 No,] M; ~∧
31.32 names?] M; ~.
31.35 once] M; one
31.35 things,] M; ~∧
31.35 aren't] arn't
31.36 crook.] M; ~∧
31.36 He] he
31.37 you're] M; your
31.37 bases] M; Bases
31.40 see] M; See
32.1 home,] ~.
32.1 find] M; Find
32.1 valuables] M; valubles
32.3 Shadow?] M; shadow∧
32.5 gentleman] M; gentle man
32.6 nervy] nervey
32.6 'em. They] M; '~∧ they

32.7 slips] M; stips
32.7 every time] M; everytime
32.8 shadow,] ~^
32.8 hey?] ~.
32.10 Holmes,] M; ~^
32.10 Bunny?] M; ~^
32.11 Carter?] ~.
32.12 Say,] M; ~^
32.16 Come,] M; ~^
32.17 Shadow!] M; ~^
32.19 Shadow!] M; shadow^
32.20 Well,] M; ~^
32.21 you're] M; your
32.24 bagful] M; bagfull
32.24 silverware] M; silver ware
32.26 say,] M; ~^
32.27 not?] ~^
32.29 tells] M; tell
*32.29 night,] M; ~^ and then
32.30 oughtn't] oughhtnt
32.30 manners?] M; ~^
32.32 back, please] M; ~^ Please
32.38 weigh?] M; ~^
32.39 punch?] M; ~.
32.40 know,] M; ~^
33.1 Say,] M; ~^
33.1 keeps?] M; keesp^
33.4 they're] M; their
33.7 Say,] M; ~^
33.8 right,] ~^
33.10 Rabies] Rabbies
33.13 Naw,] M; ~^
33.16 change?] M; ~^
33.18 scheme] M; sceme
33.20 You!] M; ~^
33.26 politics] M; polotics *also emended at 34.17; 34.21*
33.27 Say,] M; ~^
33.27 aldermen?] alderman^
33.28 Exactly,] M; ~^
33.28 capital] M; capitol

33.29 Clarence,] M; ~∧
33.30 sherry] M; Scherry
33.31 skenatcho] M; Skenatcho
33.31 sauce,] M; ~∧
33.32 remember,] M; ~∧
33.32 S-s-t] sst
33.33 what?] M; ~∧
33.34 Whist] M; whist
33.36 S-t] St
33.38 roughnecks] M; ruffnecks
34.4 *sneaks*] M; sneakes
34.6 *table*,] M; ~∧
34.7 *Rabbit's*] M; Rabbits
34.9 Well?] M; ~∧
34.10 you] M; *omitted*
34.10 here?] M; ~.
34.16 here?] M; ~∧
34.18 Rabbit!] M; ~∧
34.22 now,] ~∧
34.30 You're] M; Your
34.30-31 alderman,] ~∧
34.32 Sometimes] M; Somtimes
34.33 Gosh! You] M; ~∧ you
34.38 alderman∧] ~.
34.38 and] M; And
34.38 politician] M; polotician *also emended at 48.18*
34.39 Well,] M; ~∧
34.39 you?] M; ~.
34.39 You're] M; Your
35.2 Shadow"] M; shadow∧
35.2 card?] M; ~.
35.5 am,] M; ~∧
35.6 you're] M; your
35.7 it,] M; ~∧
35.7 why,] M; ~∧
35.11 house∧ and] M; ~. And
35.12 "House] M; — ~
35.12 Connage,] ~∧
35.12 children,] M; ~∧
35.13 twenty-two] M; ~∧~

35.13	respectively,] respecptivlyʌ
35.14	housekeeper."] M; ~ʌ —
35.15	acquainted] M; aqainted
35.16	Yes,] M; ~ʌ
35.17	meanwhile,] ~ʌ
35.17	course,] ~ʌ
35.17	you'll] you'lll
35.25	*outside*] M; out side
35.26	Beverly,] M; ~ʌ
35.30	Ah,] M; ~ʌ
35.30	evening,] M; ~ʌ
35.33	Howdy] Howde
35.34	Connage?] M; ~ʌ
35.36	Connage?] M; Connagʌ
35.38	me?] M; ~ʌ
35.39	precisely] M; precisly
36.2	you?] M; ~ʌ
36.6	house?] M; housʌ
36.7	(*Aside to Rabbit.*)] M; *omitted*
36.7	ʌLie] M; (lie
36.8	out.] M; ~)
36.9	he?] M; ~ʌ
36.10	pie-eyed] M; pieʌ eyed
36.13	eyes?] M; ~ʌ
36.15	eye?] M ~.
36.15	him?] M; ~.
36.16	Well,] M; ~ʌ
36.16	himself?] M; ~ʌ
36.22	(*Aside.*)] M; *omitted*
36.23	heavens] M; heavans
36.23	he?] M; ~ʌ
36.24	Why he's] Why Hes
36.28	none. Will] ~ʌ will
36.28	do?] M; ~ʌ
36.35	it,] M; ~ʌ
36.35	us,] M; ~ʌ
37.3	you. But] M; ~ʌ but
37.5	cartridges] M; cartriges
37.5	much!] M; ~ʌ
37.6	cartridges. They] cartrigesʌ they

37.7 matter.] M; ~∧
37.9 step. Think.] ~∧ think∧
37.11 tomorrow] M; tommorrow
*37.18 *door.)*] M; door ∧∧ and
37.19 Connage,] M; ~∧
37.20 policemen] M; policeman
37.21 They're] there
37.22 thief] M; theif
37.22 house?] M; hous∧
37.23 Where, where?] M; ~∧ Where∧
37.24 do?] ~∧
37.27 C.:] S.∧
37.29 Sir, there's] ~∧ Theres
37.29-30 house. We] M; ~∧ we
37.32 Nevertheless,] M; Never the less∧
37.35 If you] M; ~ ~ *underlined*
37.35 him—] M; ~ ?
37.35 Leon!] M; ~∧
37.36 *Dureal*] M; Duval
37.37 Oui, oui,] ~∧ Oui∧
37.38 the∧ stairs!] M; ~, ~∧
37.38 Marshal] M; marshall
37.38 inmates] M; innates
37.39 believe] M; beleive
37.39 that] M; than
38.3 Terrible!] M; ~∧
38.4 Awful!] M; ~∧
38.5 OUTSIDE] out side
38.5 thief. After] ~∧ after
38.10 stairs,] M; ~∧
*38.10-11 gen d'armes] *stet*
38.12 stairs] M; staires
38.16 burglar!] M; ~∧
38.16 *Etc.*] ect∧
38.17 *once,*] ~∧
38.19 fix,] M; ~∧
38.21 probably] M; probbably
38.24 about?] M; ~.
38.24 Why,] M; ~∧
38.25 Connage?] M; Conage∧

38.26 Yes,] M; ~∧
38.26 Mr.—Mr.—?] ~.∧ ~∧ —?
38.27 Johnston.] ~∧
38.30 is,] M; ~∧
38.32 see. What] ~∧ what
38.34 twenty-second,] M; ~∧ ~∧
38.36 Well,] M; ~∧
38.37 No,] M; ~∧
38.37 twenty-two—] M; ~∧ ~∧
38.39 twenty-two] M; ~∧~
38.39 April∧—May—] M; ~,—~∧
39.1 Why,] M; ~∧
39.3 No,] M; ~∧
39.3 fashioned] fashiond
39.3 Instead] M; Insted
39.4 "April] M; ∧~
39.4 May,"] M; ~∧∧
39.4 "April-May."] ∧~-~.∧
39.4 Like,] M; ~∧
39.5 instance,] ~∧
39.5 "April,] ∧~∧
39.5 June,] M; ~∧
39.5 March."] ~.∧
39.7 understand,] M; ~∧
39.11 I? Split] ~∧ split
39.12 twenty-one;] M; ~∧ ~∧
39.12 two—] M; ~∧
39.12-13 fourteen,] M; ~∧
39.13 you?] M; ~∧
39.16 persuade] M; persude
39.16 you?] M; ~.
39.17 comfortable—] M; ~.
39.17 *falls*] M; fall
39.18 wasn't∧?] M; wasn't,?
39.20 "Alexander's Ragtime Band"] ∧Alexander∧s rag time band∧
39.21 here—] M; ~∧
39.24 anyways] any ways
39.25 OUTSIDE] M; out side
39.25 Shadow!] M; show.

39.26 doing here?] ~ ~∧
39.27 be∧—] M; ~?—
39.29 guess∧] M; ~—
39.29 now,] M; ~∧
39.29 Shadow,] M; shadow∧
39.39 down.] ~∧
40.1 fiancée,] fiancee∧
40.3 wasn't] M; waesnt
40.4 heavens!] M; heavans∧
40.4 you] M; y
40.9 much. And] M; ~∧ and
40.10 week?] M; ~∧
40.12 drunk,] M; ~∧
40.12 man's] M; mans
40.12 derby,] M; ~∧
40.14 beard?] M; ~∧
40.15 compliment] M; complement
40.16 Anyways,] ~∧
40.19 Remember,] M; ~∧
40.23 here—] M; ~∧
40.25 Yes,] M; ~∧
40.27 impossibility] M; impossiblity
40.31 Now,] ~∧
40.32 before] M; befor
41.1 Why,] M; ~∧
41.5 detective,] M; ~∧
41.6 detective,] M; ~∧
41.9 Papier] Paper
41.9 maché?] M; ~∧
41.10 assistance] M; assisance
41.11 Ah,] M; ~∧
41.12 burglar,] M; ~∧
41.15 piece] M; peice
41.15 careful] M; carful
41.18 onto] M; on to
41.19 Still,] M; ~∧
*41.22 *from case on wall*] M; out of wall
41.23 remember,] ~∧
41.24 come,] M; ~∧
41.24 have] *omitted*

41.25 Connage's] M; Connages
41.25 assistant] M; assistent
41.25 Remember,] M; Rembember
41.26 probably] M; probablyly
41.27 How] how
41.27 women's] womans
41.27 bureau] beareau
41.31 passwords] M; pass words
41.33 *Shadow*] Shadow *above* Hart
41.35 Gentlemen,] ~∧
41.35 son. Why] M; ~∧ why
41.35 they're] M; there
41.40 you?] M; ~∧
42.1 foremost] M; formost
42.1 women's] womens
42.4 crazy!] M; ~∧
42.6 league] M; leage
42.8 Saunders, release] M; Sauders ∧ Release
42.8 once] M; one
42.10 indeed!] M; ~∧
42.11 this?] M; ~.
42.12 necessary] nessesary
42.13 friend] M; firend
42.16 explanations.] ~∧
42.17 what?] M; ~∧
42.19 Heavens! Can] M; Heavans, can
42.19 something?] M; ~∧
42.20 too] M; to
42.25 Beverly!] M; ~∧
42.26 Why,] M; ~∧
42.26 about?] M; ~.
42.26 pistol!] M; ~∧
42.29 you're] your
42.30 matter?] M; ~.
42.32 Shot?] M; ~.
42.32 him?] M; ~.
42.35 league] M; leage
42.36 rascal,] ~∧
42.36 you!] M; ~∧
42.37 something?] M; ~∧

42.38	*Voices*] M; Voice
43.2	*policemen,*] ~^
43.2	*Rudd,*] ~)
43.7	this?] M; ~^
43.8	(*Pointing . . . Saunders.*)] M; *omitted*
43.9	(*Pointing . . . Connage.*)] M; *omitted*
43.12	thief] M; theif
43.13	Ah,] ~^
43.14	Who— Who—] M; ~^ ~—
43.14	do?] M; ~.
43.17	woman] M; women
43.19	Apprehend] M; Aprehend
43.20	arrest?] M; ~.
43.23	Papa!] M; ~^
43.23	Mama!] M; ~.
43.24	restored!] M; ~^
43.25	Saunders!] M; ~^
43.26	Chinyman!] ~^
43.27	Well?] M; ~^
43.28	do?] M; ~.
43.28	somebody] sombody
43.32	RABBIT] M; Rabbit *above* Rudd
43.32	shotgun] M; shot gun
43.33	You're] Your
43.35	No,] M; ~^
43.36	too?] M; ~^
43.39	Well,] M; ~^
44.1	Where? Where?] M; ~. ~,
44.3	Some one] Som One
44.3	some one] som one
44.3	else,] M; ~^
44.8	Connage,]M; ~^
44.9	Connage?] M; ~.
44.10	Lie! !] M; ~^^
44.12	*Hubert*] M; Connage
44.13	*the Shadow*] M; Hart
44.15	ACT] M; *preceded by* (Right refers to spectators right)
44.24	him] M; *omitted*
44.25	Mais . . . denoncé.] *stet*

44.26 yes] M; Yes
44.27 detective.] ~∧
44.27 Where] M; where
44.27 disappeared?] M; ~∧
44.31 before?] M; befor∧
44.33 believe] M; beleive
44.35 policemen] M; policeman
44.36 it,] ~∧
44.36 time.] M; ~∧
45.1 overcrowded] M; overcrowed
45.1 talk. Now] M; ~∧ now
45.4 us?] M; ~.
45.6 Oui . . . Paris.] *stet*
45.8 Here, here,] M; ~∧ Here∧
45.8 No] M; no
45.10 too] M; to
45.11 policemen] M; policeman
45.11 house,] M; ~∧
45.15 sure.] ~∧
45.17 *stretch*] M; strech
45.18 ivory-headed] ~∧~
45.26 mum] M; mumm
45.27 time?] M; ~∧
45.28 something] M; somthing
45.29 away,] M; ~∧
45.32 house,] M ~∧
45.34 Well,] M; ~∧
45.36 Come,] M; ~∧
45.37 *Dureal*,] M; ~∧
45.39 Hubert, Hubert,] M; ~, ~∧
46.1 yes,] M; Yes∧
46.2 recollection] M; recolection
46.5 son,] M; ~∧
46.6 shot?] M; ~.
46.11 Helen,] M; ~∧
46.11 Mother,] M; ~∧
46.12 her?] M; Her∧
46.13 you?] M; ~∧
46.16 Engaged?] M; engaged.
46.16 Why, why,] M; ~∧ Why∧

46.16 startling! But] M; ~∧ but
46.16 Helen,] M; ~∧
46.17 girl,] M; ~∧
46.17 haven't] havn't
46.18 Come,] ~∧
46.19 Hubert. Something] ~∧ somthing
46.21 it?] M; ~∧
46.24 *away*,] M; ~∧
46.24-25 *examines it*,] ~ ~∧
46.27 Ah,] M; ~∧
46.28 us,] M; ~∧
46.28 you?] M; ~∧
46.31 say,] M; ~∧
46.31 haven't] M; havnt
46.32 aldermen?] ~∧
46.33 aldermen?] ~.
46.34 was!] M; ~∧
47.1 suit? It's] ~∧ its
47.3 so?] M; ~∧
47.4 that?] M; ~∧
47.5 butler's] M; butlers
47.5 clothes] M; cloths
47.7 Cheap? Why] M; ~∧ why
47.13 Come,] ~∧
47.13 Say,] M; ~∧
47.13 house?] M; ~.
47.15 Shadow?] shadow.
47.16 they're] M; there
47.16 onto] M; on to
47.17 safely] M; saftly
47.19 (*Enter the Shadow*,)] M; *omitted*
47.21 police∧] M; ~,
47.22 weeks,] M; ~∧
47.22 Still,] M; ~∧
47.25 Still,] M; ~∧
47.26 yet,] ~∧
47.27 hundred,] ~∧
47.29 do,] M; *omitted*
47.29 Sir,] M; ~∧
47.30 brother?] M; ~.

47.30 him?] M; ~.
47.31 him?] M; ~,
47.31 Why,] why^
47.31 course,] M; ~^
47.33 house?] ~.
47.33 Shadow?] M; shadow^
47.34 it] M; It
47.36 say?] M; ~^
47.37 bullet-headed] M; ~^~
47.38 seen,] M; ~^
47.39 then,] M; ~^
47.39 him?] M; ~.
48.1 Why—] M; ~^
48.1 oh yes—] M; ~ ~^
48.1 why yes—] ~ ~^
48.1 course—] M; ~^
48.1 Why that's] M; why thats
48.2 see. It's] ~^ its
48.5 success,] ~^
48.7 disappointed] M; dissapointed
48.9 had?] M; ~.
48.12 night,] M; ~^
48.12 Johnston,] ~^
48.16 being!] M; ~^
48.18 Ah,] M; ~^
48.20 It] M; I
48.21 you,] M; ~^
48.21 sir?] M; ~^
48.23 bicycle] M; bysycle
48.26 eccentric] M; excentric
48.26 drop,] ~^
48.27 sir?] ~^
48.27 Sweets] M; sweets
48.27 sweet,"] M; ~^^
48.27 know.] M; ~"
48.29 cracked,] M; ~^
48.30 Sir,] M; ~^
48.34 What?] M; ~^
48.36 a^tellin'] a-tellin^
48.37 crushed!] M; ~^

48.37 pray,] M; ~^
48.38 heard,] M; ~^
48.39 There!] M; ~^
49.1 rubbish.] ~^
49.1 Kate,] M; ~^
49.3 up?] ~.
49.7 *followed*] M; followd
49.8 back door,] ~ ~^
49.10 out?] M; ~.
49.11 monsier] *stet*
49.12 prisoner?] ~.
49.13 I,] M; ~^
49.13 Dureal,] M; ~^
49.14 Oh,] M; ~^
49.14 Dureal?] M; ~^
49.15 What,] M; ~^
49.15 me?] M; ~^
49.16 gen d'arme] *stet*
49.17 Paris, the] M; ~. The
49.17 efficient] M; efficeint
49.19 Shadow?] M; shadow.
49.20 am,] ~^
49.21 you.] ~^
49.21 It] M; it
49.22 Monsuer] *stet*
49.25 equal] M; equeal
49.29 police] M; Police
49.29 it?] M; ~.
49.31 out?] M; ~.
49.33 cells?] M; ~.
49.34 closets?] ~^
49.37 certainly. Here] ~^ here
50.5 *policeman's*] policemans
50.7 you,] M; ~^
50.9 *father.*] ~^
50.9 He] M; he
50.11 you,] M; ~^
50.11 Shadow,] M; ~^
50.11 whatever] M; what ever
50.14 *crooks*] Crooks

50.15	Yes,] M; ~^
50.17	you're] your
50.17	burglar?] M; ~^
50.18	burglar. Me] ~^ me
50.19	cinch,] M; ~^
50.22	I'd^] M; I'd—
50.24	nonsense!] M; ~^
50.24	It's] its
50.25	me?] M; ~^
50.27	some one] somone
*50.33	*McGinness*] *omitted*
50.33	*unlocks*] M; Unlocks
50.33	*out. They*] ~^ they
50.34	*head*,] ~^
50.36	he?] M; ~^
50.37	*around*] M; round
50.37	Gone!] M; ~^
50.38	Where?] M; ~^
50.39	him!] M; ~^
51.1	me,] M; ~^
51.1	my!] M; ~^
51.6	Well?] M; ~^
51.7	Well?] M; ~^
51.10	Yes,] M; ~^
51.12	phone,] ~^
51.13	Central,] M; ~^
51.13-14	Forty-fourth Street] fourty^ fourth street
51.14	fire?] M; ~^
51.16	not?] M; ~^
51.18	Hello— Is] M; ~^ is
51.18	Forty-fourth Street] M; fourtty-fourth street
51.19	Connages'] M; Connages
51.20	Fifty-second Street] fifty-second street
51.22	*receiver*] M; reciever
51.25	scream?] M; sceeam^
51.26	to.] M; too.
51.27	Listen—] M; ~^
51.27	you?] ~.
51.28	a] M; *omitted*
51.29	steal?] M; ~.

51.30 onto] M; on to
51.30 Yes,] M; ~^
51.31 thief] M; theif
51.31 then?] M; ~.
51.33 weren't] wern't
51.34 wasn't?] ~.
51.36 is,] M; ~^
51.37 Yes,] M; ~^
51.37 out,] ~^
51.39 burglar?] M; ~^
52.1 it,] M; ~^
52.2 it?] M; ~.
52.3 you,] M; ~^
52.3 miss] Miss
52.3 a way] M; away
52.4 forfeited] M; forfieted
52.5 gentleman,] M; ~^
52.5 thing] M; think
52.6 burglar,] M; ~^
52.8 withdrawn] M; with drawn
52.8 night,] M; ~.
52.8-9 burglar,] M; ~^
52.9 *Opens*] M; Opends
52.11 goodbye?] M; good bye.
52.12 Listen—] M; ~^
52.13 tonight] M; night
52.14 was,] ~^
52.17 incompetent] incompetant
52.22 of money] to money
52.25 and—] ~^
52.31 at] that
53.4 housekeeper's] houskeepers
53.6 smoking] Smoking
53.11 Chinyman] Chinaman

Coward

Textual Commentary

Coward is extant in a transcription, in Elizabeth Magoffin's hand, with heavy cream-colored paper covers, approximately 26.4 x 21 cm., front and back. On the front cover (over the title '"COWARD"' in black ink) is pasted the 21.6 x 13.8 cm. printed program beginning '"Coward" | A comedy in two acts by Scott Fitzgerald. . . .' The play itself, all in Elizabeth Magoffin's hand in black ink with red and blue crayon markings indicating entrances and exits, etc., consists of 31 leaves, cream-colored wove paper, measuring 25.4 x 20.4 cm. Perforations at top right and left indicate that the leaves were originally attached with fasteners. Act one is paginated on rectos only [1]; 2-5; [2 inserts]; 6-12; [insert, blank except for diagonal cross]; 13-22; [insert]; 23-27; plus one final unpaginated leaf, a list of stage furnishings, property, and costumes, approximately 25.2 x 20.1 cm., poor quality white wove paper, with verso blank. Act two, written back to front on the versos of pp. 27-10 (including inserts), is paginated 28-32; [insert, blank except for diagonal cross]; 33-42; [insert]; 43-45.

In addition, there are seven unnumbered holograph leaves (all versos are blank) in pencil written by Fitzgerald after Elizabeth Magoffin had completed her transcription and then copied by her and added as inserts to the transcription. They introduce some comical dialogue and a new character, Angelina Bangs, to the original script. The holograph leaves, torn out of a small notebook, are white wove paper with blue rules and measure approximately 21.3 x 16.4 cm. At one time they were fastened with a straight pin at top left and a paper clip. They are used here as copy-text for those pages which survive; otherwise copy-text for *Coward* is the Magoffin transcription.

A facsimile of the list of stage furnishings, stage properties, and costumes, the recto of the final unpaginated leaf of the transcription, is included in this edition.

Textual Notes

59.26-27 (Repeated . . . 1913.) Written horizontally to right of cast list.

62.23-63.20 I . . . Douglas] Copy-text here is Fitzgerald's holograph headed 'Part of Angelina Bangs.' The first line, 'I . . . spirit,' is Fitzgerald's cue.

63.7 Angeline] Fitzgerald's variant spelling, possibly purposeful, has been retained here and at 72.40.

69.32 *Judge Douglas and*] Added because Judge D. must return to the stage to participate in the action following.

69.34 right pert!] Stage direction following—'(Exit Jeff)'—deleted here since Jeff must remain on stage to wheel out the Judge.

72.25, 27, 28, 29, 30, 31 liver] Magoffin's transcription reads 'liver' above 'heart,' the two bracketed. In some instances, 'liver' and the brace are in slightly darker ink, suggesting that they were added later. Fitzgerald's cue to his holograph insert that follows ('End of liver scene') suggests his preference.

72.33-73.11 *Enter* . . . line."] Copy-text here is Fitzgerald's holograph with the exception of 'I . . . *Jeff*' (73.4-8) from Magoffin's transcription. This complies with Fitzgerald's instructions in his holograph—'Jeff wheel me (etc) Exit Judge'—to insert 'I . . . *Jeff*.' 'I . . . *Jeff*' are the original lines Magoffin later deleted rather than those that she copied in her insert to the transcription, with 'I say' (73.6) and '*growling*' (73.8) omitted.

73.4-8 I . . . *Jeff*] See previous note.

84.2 Come . . . garden.] Copy-text is cue line of Fitzgerald's holograph.

84.3 *flits*] See following note.

84.3-4 (*She* . . . *flitting*.)] '(*She* . . . *her*)' is from Magoffin's original transcription; '(*Percy* . . . *flitting*)' is from the insert in her hand. In the original transcription, the direction '(She flits out, and Percy very awkwardly "flits" after her)' just precedes the direction to insert. Since the couple remains on stage, 'out' has been deleted here.

84.5-19 (*Enter* . . . (*Exit*.)] Copy-text here is Fitzgerald's holograph.

84.20 (*Enter*] Preceding '(Exit Percy and Virginia)' in Magoffin transcription deleted here since their exit in insert occurs earlier.

Editorial Emendations in the Copy-Text

59.1	^*Coward*^] "Coward"
59.27	evening,] ~^
60.3	*colonial*] Colonial
60.13	able-bodied] able^ bodied
60.14	I'd] I'ld *also emended at 64.4; 66.10; 68.11; 68.27; 70.17; 72.2; 72.7*
60.18	she'd] she'ld *also emended at 60.21; 66.28*
62.1	lady] Lady *also emended at 84.26 and 84.31*
62.14	Ashton,] ~^
62.15	father's] Father's
62.15	Governor^] Gov.
62.16	New^ York^] N. Y.
62.23	they've] M; the've
62.24	*Bangs*] M; omitted
62.28	So?] M; ~^
62.30	it?] M; ~^
62.31	namesake,] M; ~^
62.31	friend] M; freind
62.33	book!] M; ~^
62.34	dry! !] M; ~^ ^
62.35	Lindy,] M; ~^
62.38	creature!] M; ~^
62.39	Cecilia! !] M; ~^^
63.1	learn,] M; ~^
63.2	girl,] M; ~^
63.3	something] M; somthing
63.3	practice,] M; ~^
63.4	sanctimonious] M; santimonius
63.5	I,] M; ~^
63.5	alas,] M; ~^
63.5	struggles.] M; ~^
63.6	father's] fathers
63.6	family,] M; ~^
*63.7	Angeline] *stet; also at 72.40*
63.7	overcome] M; over come
63.8	Alas,] M; ~^
63.8	overcomes] M; over comes

63.9 shame—] M; ~∧
63.9 "Rats!"] M; ∧~∧∧
63.10 ill-natured] M; ill∧ natured
63.11 win?] M; ~∧
63.14 going,] M; ~∧
63.14 Goodbye] M; Good bye *also emended at 75.29 (2x)*
63.14 Children,] M; ~∧
63.17 sanctimonious] M; sanctimonius
63.17 creature!] M; ~∧
63.20 Douglas] M; Douglass (Ect)
63.31 all right] Alright *also emended at 69.35*
63.32 he'd] he'ld
64.37 mother] Mother *also emended at 77.8*
64.39 father] Father *also emended at 65.38; 66.35; 70.30*
65.30(2x) fathah] Fathah
65.30 —yoh] —you
66.20 you'd] you'ld
67.10 goodbye] good bye
67.23 Early's] Earley's
67.27 Celia,] ~∧
68.2-3 Lieutenant] Lieut. *also emended at 68.7*
69.7 sister] Sister *also emended at 69.14*
69.14 There,] ~∧
69.18 cane] cain
69.19 all right] alright *second l interlined above; also emended at 69.20*
*69.32 *Judge Douglas and*] *omitted*
*69.34 right pert!] ~~! (Exit Jeff)
70.36 rode] road
70.41 greenbacks] green backs
72.6 south] South *also emended at 75.28*
*72.25 liver] liver *interlined above* heart *with the two words bracketed; also emended at 72.27; 72.28; 72.29; 72.30; 72.31*
72.34 disagreement? How] M; ~∧ how
72.36 this?] M; ~∧
72.36 you,] M; ~∧
72.36 lady,] M; ~∧

72.37 house?] M; house∧
72.38 slow,] M; ~∧
72.39 it?] M; ~∧
72.39 I?] M; ~∧
72.40 There.] ~∧
72.40 it.] ~∧
72.40-41 victorious] M; victorius
73.1 this?] ~∧
73.1 Bangs,] M; ~∧
73.1 Angelina?] M; ~∧
73.3 me. And] M; ~∧ and
73.3-4 (*turning to Jim*),] M; *omitted*
73.4 you're] your
73.4 pair—] pair— Jeff wheel me (ect) Exit Judge
*73.4-8 I . . . *Jeff*)] M; *omitted*
73.4 control] controle
73.6 going!—] ~!∧
73.11 (*Sings.*)] M; *omitted*
73.38 sergeant] sargeant
74.20 Charley,] ~∧
74.28 beggar] begger
75.22 mad,] ~∧
75.23 Lindy?] ~.
78.3 protégé] protegé
78.25 was] was was
79.18 Mother,] ~∧
79.18-19 economizing] enonomizing
80.35 Chickamauga] Chicamauga
81.7 *Starts*] Startes
81.25 He'd] He'ld
84.2 rose] M; Rose
*84.3 *flits*] flits out
84.6 Unchaperoned!] M; Unchaperond∧
84.8 terrible!] M; ~∧
84.8 Blush,] M; ~∧
84.8 lady,] M; ~∧
84.9 it?] ~∧
84.10 you're] M; your
84.13 authorities] authorites
84.15 this."] ~∧∧

84.16	"A] M; ^~
84.17	account—"] M; ~^^
*84.20	(*Enter*] (Exit Percy and Virginia) (Enter
84.20	—*Privates*] (Privates
84.20	*Barkis*—] Barkis)
85.14	*ammunition*] amunition
85.15	ammunition] amunition
85.20	peaceably] peacably

End-of-Line Hyphenation

76.35	schoolhouse
79.32	somehow

Assorted Spirits

Textual Commentary

The only available text for *Assorted Spirits*, and, thus, the copy-text for this edition, is a typescript with revisions in at least two different hands, one of which is Elizabeth Magoffin's. In addition, Elizabeth Magoffin's signature appears in two places, the top margin at the beginning of each act of the typescript. Nothing, however, is in Fitzgerald's hand. At least two typewriters were used in transcribing the play, one for each act. It is not possible to identify the typist or typists; Fitzgerald is not known to have typed. In addition, from the many comma splices, all uncharacteristic of Elizabeth Magoffin's transcriptions, as well as from the absence of certain capitalized proper nouns and of semicolons followed by capitalized words, both characteristic of her transcriptions and of one of the inserts of this play in her hand, it seems unlikely that she was the typist.

The typescript is in covers, front and rear, yellowed frayed wove leaves, measuring approximately 30.5 x 22 cm. Pasted on the front is the printed program, 22.9 x 15.3 cm. headed ' "Assorted Spirits" | A Comedy in Two Acts by Scott Fitzgerald,' listing cast, etc. The first leaf, white wove paper, 28 x 21.8 cm., 'Union Bond' watermark, is in Elizabeth Magoffin's hand in black ink and lists title and cast, etc. The verso has blue rules, the rules beginning below a 'Douglas Lodge | Itasca State Park' letterhead. The remainder of the letterhead includes place and date, 'Arago, Minn., —191 .' The date has not been filled in. This leaf has a perforation at top center where it was once fastened to the remaining leaves of the typescript, each of which has perforations at the top. Act one consists of 21 leaves, and, except for inserts, all are white wove paper, all measure approximately 27.8 x 21.5 cm.; all have 'HAMMERMILL STERLING BOND' watermark; all are typed black carbon copies, elite type; many have corrections in black ink (some over pencil) and pencil; many have red and yellow markings for entrances, exits, etc.; and all versos are blank. The leaves are foliated 1-6; [7]; 8-10; [2 inserts, blue ruled white wove paper with punched holes for a ring binder, 26.2 x 20 cm., in Elizabeth Magoffin's hand in black ink mostly over pencil (versos are blank)]; 11-13;

[2 inserts in Elizabeth Magoffin's hand in black ink, both on paper similar to the first leaf (with 'Douglas Lodge' letterhead on verso)]; 14; [15]; 16; [17]. Act two consists of 16 leaves, white wove paper, measuring approximately 27.8 x 21.5 cm. (all versos are blank), all with 'HAMMERMILL STERLING BOND' watermark, many with corrections in black ink, some over pencil, and many with red markings for entrances and exits, etc. The leaves are foliated 1-6 (typescript pica black ribbon); 7-16 (black carbon, pica type).

The inserts in the typescript were an attempt to clarify one of the subplots, the theft of the money. In the original version, Josephus Hendrix agrees to purchase the Wetherby house for ten thousand dollars if Mr. Wetherby proves that it is not haunted. Later on in this version, a thief, Ev (an early name for Second Story Salle), appears on stage counting the money. But she is startled when she sees Will Chapman, in the house by mistake and in a devil's costume. Ev drops the money and flees, and Will leaves, too, upon hearing Hulda, the maid, approach. Hulda then takes the money and exits, and, immediately after, young Dick Wetherby enters and announces that the money is missing. But since there was no reason in the script for Dick to be aware of this, and further, no identification of Ev or how she got the money in the first place, much of this would have been puzzling to the audience. Thus a number of script changes were made.

First Mr. Hendrix was shown entrusting Dick with the money. At the same time, an insert was added showing Salle (Ev's new name) telling Hulda of her plan to take the money from Dick's room. Then another change in script occurred. A direction was added showing Salle picking Dick's pocket on stage. This direction was further amplified in a second insert with Salle's masquerading as Minnie Maddern Fiske, distracting Dick, and taking the money. Unfortunately, the first insert, with its allusion to the robbery in Dick's room, was never corrected. And neither was Dick's remark in act two about the money having been taken from his room.

TEXTUAL NOTES

91.1-31 *Assorted . . . uniforms.*] In Elizabeth Magoffin's hand.
93.26 are] original typescript reading 'I am' was changed (in

Elizabeth Magoffin's hand) to 'you are only' when speech ('The . . . art.') originally assigned to Dick was assigned to Mr. W. The redundant second 'only' was probably added erroneously and is deleted in this edition.

96.35 (*Calls.*)] Added to indicate that Will's aunt is not on stage.

99.34-100.18 (*Window . . . Will.*)] Insert in Elizabeth Magoffin's hand.

102.17-103.34 (*Enter . . . rush.*)] An insert in Elizabeth Magoffin's hand partly replaces the following lines from the typescript, some of which, from an even earlier version of the play, have been erroneously left undeleted; the alterations in the following section are in Magoffin's hand, and, unless otherwise noted, in black ink over pencil.

(S. S. S. holds up Dick and picks pocket) (Enter Ev, carrying bank notes in her hand, goes to light and counts them.)

S. S. S. Not a 'arf bad deal. Ten thousand cold, crisp bills! (Faints while Dick goes for water. S. S. S. sees Will peep out of closet, screams, drops bank notes and jumps out of window.)

(Enter Hulda, she picks up money.)

Hul What's this? *The* $10,000. Second Story Salle must have dropped it (Exit.)

Dick (Coming in.) My Lord. Someone's taken that ten thousand dollars. What a mess I'm in. I mustn't let anyone know. I'll—I'll search the house. (Exit.)

1 (S. S. S. . . . pocket)] *interlined above; followed by* 'insert' *(circled) in black ink*

2-3 (Enter . . . them.)] *erroneously left undeleted*

4 S. S. S.] *interlined in black ink above black ink deleted* 'Ev'

4 crisp bills!] *interlined above deleted* ''ard round dollars.'

5-6 (Faints . . . screams,] *interlined in black ink above ink deleted* '(Enter Will. Ev sees him, screams,'

8 (Enter] *preceded by black ink deleted* 'Will hears someone coming. Exits.'; *following parenthesis added in black ink*

9 What's . . . Salle] *interlined above and below deleted* 'Someone' *with brace pointing to* 'Hul'

10 (Exit.)] *followed in right margin by* 'Insert' *circled, all in pencil and then erased*

11 Lord] *interlined above deleted* 'God!'

Lines 103.22-26 '(*S. S. S. . . . Exit.*)' have been retained here from the typescript and replace the insert's single direction, '(Exit S. S. S. through window)'. This direction is not sufficient for references later in the play to Salle's dropping the money after seeing Will in costume and Hulda's finding the money and keeping it; both actions must occur on stage at this point. Further, 'What . . . house.' (103.33-34), clarifying Dick's later surreptitious actions, also has been retained from the typescript. See "Textual Commentary."

104.30 no.] Lack of capitalization may indicate a lowering of voice, reflecting Mr. Wetherby's fear.

106.5 (*Aside.*) Added to present edition. Probably erroneously omitted since entire line was inserted later and occurs immediately after previous aside. Without this direction and the next one added, this aside and the following statement (spoken to the others) are contradictory and make no sense.

106.5 (*To others.*)] See previous textual note.

106.36 Well . . . me—] Originally assigned erroneously to Miss Spigot. In the typescript, this line is contiguous with Miss Spigot's previous speech as well as with the previous stage direction. To correct this, 'Hul' was written in left margin above deleted typed 'Hul' and to left of '*it.*) . . . me—' (106.35-36).

110.29 (*Clara*] Beginning of carbon typescript.

115.21-22 Ta-ta— . . . *her.*)] Retained here despite possible redundancy resulting from later insertion of "I'll . . . *haste.*)' (115.17-21) added along right margin in Elizabeth Magoffin's hand.

Editorial Emendations in the Copy-Text

91.1 ‸*Assorted Spirits*‸] "Assorted Spirits"
91.16 *hypochondriac*] hypocondriac
91.25 MADAME] Madam
91.29 *Same*] Sam
92.1 ACT I] *omitted*
92.18 mind;] ~,

93.15	of] *omitted*
93.21	continually.] *followed in typescript below and to left by* Dick *(speech heading) preceding deleted line*
* 93.26	are] are only
93.28	babble] bable
94.22	to.] *followed in typescript in right margin by* telephone *(underlined twice) in pencil*
94.32	Joseph] *stet*
94.36	beds∧] ~,
94.36	back.] *followed in typescript in right margin by* door *(underlined twice) in pencil*
94.40	"Hey"] ∧~∧
95.19	reader—hm] ~∧~
96.12	Exactly.] ~,
96.22	*the*] *preceded in typescript in left margin by* door *(underlined twice) in pencil*
* 96.35	(*Calls.*)] *omitted*
97.15	see∧] ~,
98.30	expect;]~∧
99.27	it] *omitted*
99.27	safekeeping] safe Keeping
101.25	thinks] things
101.32	*exits*] exit
*102.17-103.34	(*Enter . . . rush.*)] *insert only partly replaces typescript: see "Textual Commentary" and "Textual Notes"*
102.19	evening] Evening
103.6	primitive] primative
*104.30	no.] *stet*
104.32	Whew,] ~∧
105.30	police,] ~∧
105.32-33	*candlestick*] candle stick
*106.5	(*Aside.*)] *omitted*
*106.5	(*To others.*)] *omitted*
106.14	(*Curtain.*)] *omitted*
109.4	breathe] breath *also emended at 109.5*
112.1	'ave] ∧~

112.20 oh Salle!] ~~^
112.21 Where . . . here.] *interlined as* in here^ Where shall I put this money? I'll put it
112.24 *clothes,* ^*opposite door.*] clothes. (opposite door)
112.31 pressers] presser's
113.12 Goodbye] Good bye
113.21 get] get get
114.21 1ST] Lst
115.4 is] *omitted*
115.9 penitentiary] penentiary
*115.21-22 Ta-ta— . . . *her.*)] *stet*
116.36 Lord! (*Exit.*)] lord! (Exit^)

WORD DIVISION IN THIS VOLUME

In quotations from the present edition, no line-end hyphens are to be retained since none of the end-line hyphenation reflects the copy-text.